SIGNS OF LITERATURE

Language, Ideology and the Literary Text

Kenneth James Hughes

Talonbooks   •   Vancouver   •   1986

published with assistance from the Canada Council and the Manitoba Arts Council

Talonbooks
201 / 1019 East Cordova Street
Vancouver
British Columbia V6A 1M8
Canada

Typeset in Times by Resistance Graphics; printed and bound in Canada by Hignell Printing Ltd.

First printing: October 1986

Canadian Cataloguing in Publication Data

Hughes, Kenneth James, 1932-
   Signs of literature

   Bibliography: p.
   ISBN 0-88922-236-3

   1. English language - Style. 2. English
language - Semantics. 3. Figures of speech.
4. English literature - History and criticism.
I. Title.
PE1421.H84 1986   820'.9   C86-091451-8

54,831

CONTENTS

Part II: Application of Elements of Prose Criticism

PREFACE

This text is only a quasi-linear text and will no doubt infuriate those possessed of a strictly linear consciousness, as will the numerous repetitions. However, the many repetitions have a pedagogical function based on the practice of teaching first-year college and other students, for whom the text is intended. This taught me that constant repetition of a new consciousness is the only way to dislodge the firmly entrenched errors which structure an old consciousness. The text can be entered at any point and read in any order.

One of the most common objections to enterprises of this kind is that they involve the use of "jargon". There are several responses that can be made to this objection.

1) We must have names not only to be able to discuss phenomema, but also to be able to see them. Not to have names means that we cannot discuss phenomena. Not to discuss phenomena relating to an object under scrutiny means to conceal or to be blind to those phenomena. To conceal or to be blind to those phenomena means to avoid scrutinizing the object as a totality. Avoiding scrutiny of the total object reveals some form of ideologically conditioned repression. Guilty of all these things, traditional criticism stands condemned by its own charge of jargon.

2) The additions to the critical vocabulary of literature, made in recent times and used below, come mainly from Greek and Latin, and are no more strange than the other Greek and Latin terms which we are familiar with, such as metaphor and metonymy.

3) The charge of "jargon" comes from those who favour the "plain prose discourse," those who erroneously assume that discourse to be "natural", and a style laden with critical terms to be "unnatural". This view is completely wrong. The plain prose style is not some natural, transparent, ideologically neutral conveyer of the TRUTH, but is currently the most ideological form of any conceivable discourse, for it claims neutrality and naturalness, when in fact it is as cultural a construction as any other form of discourse. The so-called jargon-laden style quite deliberately dislocates the plain prose style to keep the reader aware of its own constructed nature. It does not wish to hide its materiality in order to appear like a set of clean ideas coming from nowhere. Rather it says to the reader, "I am a construction, an attempt at understanding, not THE TRUTH, so read me with care and take whatever you find useful". The charge of jargon convicts those who make it, for even

as they make the charge they hide something: the materiality of their own constructed discourse.

The book was written without institutional aid of any kind, and in the face of some serious academic bureaucratic obstructions (not at the College). I am nonetheless thankful for the help of some very active people around me at St. John's College: Dennis Cooley (English), David Arnason (English), Dawne McCance (Religion), and Alfred Shepherd (Psychology); to Al Pressey (Psychology) for the loan of books, Aubrey Neale (History), and to Barry Rutland of Carleton University for a long and detailed critique of earlier drafts along with extended conversations. My debts to old and new masters will be obvious, though the text is not without its own contributions. I can hardly fail to thank Karl Siegler, Murray Madryga and Mary Schendlinger, whose editorial skills and courtesy I pushed to the limits. What can one say of such people?

PART I
LANGUAGE, IDEOLOGY AND THE LITERARY TEXT

Language and Literature in Our Time

This is a text on the subject of language and literature for general readers, along with those entering university. Of necessity, it cannot be complete for at least six major reasons:

1) While language and literature stand complete at any one time, their momentary completeness in an open-ended process of change means that some event such as a new word or a new work will make them different for us by tomorrow;

2) Any attempt at fullness, this side of the impossible completeness, would require many volumes, and go beyond the desired level of a primer text;

3) Literary methodology has entered a state of severe crisis, as the following pages will indicate, and the revolution has by no means yet begun to run its course;

4) Twentieth-century literature itself is in severe crisis, and shows no signs of restabilization;

5) As we shall see, the lines between fiction and non-fiction begin to blur as the various revolutions proceed;

6) We have yet to assess the full import of the discourse of advertising,

television, film, the "media" in general, on literary and linguistic changes in our day.

It may well be that transformed literary studies, along the broad lines proposed below, will become a vital prerequisite for citizenship, even sanity, in the emerging world of the late twentieth century. We shall begin to make this point here by indicating some blurring of commonly held distinctions between reportage or non-fiction prose, and literary forms, or fiction.

The Language of *Time*

To accurately see the blurring of lines between non-fiction and fiction, we shall examine briefly the deceptively simple-looking cover and the accompanying page of content from *TIME* magazine of March 25, 1985, the week that announced the appointment of the new Soviet leader, Mikhail Gorbachev.

The Portrait in *Time*

The cover for the Gorbachev *TIME* issue presents a head and shoulders portrait of an inscrutable near-smiling Gorbachev on the right. On the left we meet the negative space of white words which appear through a grey-green-blue colour, and read: "Moscow's New Boss—Younger, Smoother and Probably Formidable". So conditioned have we become to the naive realist error which takes the image (here the painting of Gorbachev) to be the thing itself (the man), that we typically look at this portrait, then proceed to the article. There we expect to find a verbal report or description of the real visual thing we have just seen: Gorbachev. After all, as our culture of the gaze and the spectacle tells us, a picture is worth a thousand words. In fact, this cover portrait turns out to be a printed colour photograph of a visual artist's free rendition, in the form of a painting, of an original photograph or photographs of Gorbachev. That realization takes us a very long way from the real thing which this striking realist cover illustration asserts itself to be. *TIME* gives us not Gorbachev, then, but Gorbachev seen from a specific point of view; the point of view, of course, of *TIME*. We know this situation to be so because of the remarkable alignment between the printed colour photograph of a painting of a photograph or photographs, and the accompanying verbal text of *TIME*, itself a verbal construct, not a visual one. What either the illustration of the painting or the verbal text has to do with Gorbachev himself, finally, we do not and cannot know. This is because, as *TIME* keeps telling us, he is a mystery man.

Time Constitutes Gorbachev

We only know what *TIME* (or any other medium) tells us, and therefore *TIME* (in this case) constitutes Gorbachev for us. *TIME* makes us see him in a single way. And since most other sources in the West know as little as *TIME* does about Gorbachev, the influential view of *TIME* will not likely be contradicted. We have, therefore, in this edition of *TIME*, a coherent and consistent portrait of Gorbachev that works perfectly well as a piece of interrelated visual art and verbal fiction. We have no way of knowing or verifying, however, how well these visual and verbal textual constructions of Gorbachev match the "significatum", the empirical object of reference, which is that Russian man, Gorbachev. *TIME* may be more or less right, or accidentally or wilfully wrong, we simply cannot know. What we can know, and what we shall now see, is that *TIME*'s visual and verbal text is not objective reportage, but a literary construct in the manner of prose fiction.

The Markets of *Time*

As a mass circulation magazine in a market-oriented capitalist society, *TIME* captures and influences as many readers as possible. On that subject it has no choice because of the objective, competitive conditions under which it operates. It must generate audiences to succeed, to continue, and it must at least cover costs, while ideally in this system it should also make a profit. To make a profit, *TIME* must produce large audiences; first, for the subscription income and, second, for the high income it must attract from advertisers who wish to attract that same audience. For, contrary to the common view which sees the various media selling space to advertisers, their practice in fact involves the selling of guaranteed audiences of certain kinds and sizes under certain conditions, to advertisers.

The Readers of *Time*

TIME recognizes that ours is a society of fragments in which reading, for most people, is something done between one significant past activity and an impending significant future one, as for example between arriving at the dentist's office and getting into her chair. For this reason, *TIME* designs its editions to be read selectively or as a whole, in one or many settings or sittings, for shorter or longer periods of time, and in any order. *TIME* has basically two audiences: those who read the whole of *TIME*, and those who read parts only. Both these audiences have in common the typical practice of reading the headings to articles, even if they do not intend to read specific articles. *TIME* therefore works especially hard to make these very skilfully created headings function as microcosms of the macrocosmic articles in question. By this means, *TIME* aims to ensure that the essence of the whole communication gets through whether readers read the article which accompanies the headings, or not. This means that *TIME* will attempt to constitute Gorbachev as a certain type in the minds of all its readers. We have already passed by a version of this transaction on the front cover.

The Cover and Text of *Time*

On the front cover of the Gorbachev edition, the sign sequence "Moscow's New Boss" suggests power unified in one person. The succeeding signs, "Younger, Smoother", imply a surface appearance, the term "smoother" moving beyond the descriptive "younger" to a value judgment. This value judgment implies ambiguously that there might be something beneath the surface, that this man may be an "operator". The conjunction "and" then prepares the way for a clearer suggestion of this something beneath the surface: "And Probably Formidable". The verbal text on the cover thus matches the visual image of a single man to suggest a smooth surface; and powerful, but enigmatic, depths. The interior verbal text fills out this dualist vision.

If we now turn to that text in the interior, we discover that the signs on the front cover serve as thematic statements which find development in that text. "Moscow's New Boss" from the cover enters the interior text in the statement: "Though Gorbachev may exhibit a more amiable personality than his predecessors, there is no doubt that he is cut from the same ideological cloth...", this "Younger" leader then becomes "exemplar of the New Guard", and "the first Soviet leader born after the 1917 Bolshevik Revolution". This "Smoother" man "can apparently mask his feelings when the occasion calls for it", and indeed "Gorbachev's trip to Britain was even more successful in putting a human face on the Soviet leadership". This "probably formidable" apparatchik emerges as "a cool reflective man quite capable of a steely riposte" and his "rapid rise through party ranks suggests an adroit politician who has been able to advance under leaders as different in style as Brezhnev and Andropov". Finally, the dualist vision informs the whole *TIME* text, as some of the above quotations will have suggested, with mentions of the superficial "public affability" of a man who "delighted British hosts with his banter", but who deep down remains "totally a product of his party's system". We shall return to this dualist vision of the main text.

The Under- and Overdetermined Discourse of *Time*

Both these forms of discourse appear in *TIME*. DISCOURSE refers in this instance to the uses to which language may be put, be it poetry or prose, fiction or non-fiction, or what we call overdetermined or underdetermined. To understand how the headings in the *TIME* text work we must first distinguish underdetermined from overdetermined discourse. The subject will be dealt with more fully throughout this text, but for now UNDERDETERMINED DISCOURSE refers to the plain prose style that arose in the early seventeenth century, to be legitimized by the Royal Society of London on its foundation in 1662, as the language of science. This plain prose style emphasized the linear (syntagmatic) syntax (syntax=the order of signs in sequences): the conceptually horizontal subject-verb-object sentence. It sought to ban metaphor, and aspired to the condition of logic, searching for mathematical precision. In the semiotic terms to be developed in this book, however, all language consists of sequences of basic sign units. Signs are binary (L. *binarius*=in two parts) in structure. They have a material SIGNIFIER (the sounds "d-o-g" uttered, or the material black marks "dog" written on a page) and a mental SIGNIFIED (the concept generated by the material signifier). Underdetermined discourse seeks to suppress any sense of the material signifiers. It represses the materiality of language in order to make the sequence of signified concepts appear like pure and disembodied ideas. It further seeks to make the signified concepts stand for, or represent, things. In this way the textual world created by underdetermined discourse appears to become the exact naive realist equivalent of the empirical world about which it purports to speak. In short, underdetermined discourse claims to be the language of Truth. Moreover, it does so in a context which would deny truth value to other forms of discourse, such as prose fiction and poetry. Revolutions in our understanding of language in the twentieth century have undermined the illusion that underdetermined discourse can be a privileged form of discourse with sole access to The Truth.

By contrast, OVERDETERMINED DISCOURSE refers to the discourse of literature, of fiction. We call it overdetermined because in addition to dealing with the conceptual side of language through sequences of signifieds, it also deliberately uses—indeed even flaunts—the material signifiers themselves.

The headings in the *TIME* article, and much of the article itself, are examples of the overdetermined discourse of literature or fiction, not the plain prose underdetermined discourse of science and so-called objective reportage. Here we meet the blurring of distinctions between poetry and historical narrative. We discover this immediately through the appearance of the literary device of alliteration, the repetition of initial consonant sounds, which links different signs into clusters to create special effects. For example, notice the alliteration of "s":

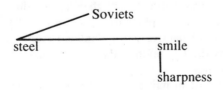

11

This practice foregrounds the cluster of "s" signs against the background of the other signs to cause them to say, beyond the reach of conventional consciousness, that "Soviets=steel—smile—sharpness". The repeated definite article in "The Soviets=the smile" aids this foregrounding process. And again, we find alliteration linking Gorbachev with the steel smile sequence through "Glints":

Glints

Gorbachev

In this process we have seen the main heading establish the genus "Soviets", then subsidiary headings establish Gorbachev as species of this genus, finally coming round full circle to set up Gorbachev as a leader, or type, as the genus itself.

CONSONANCE, the repetition of other than initial consonant sounds, also helps this foregrounding as we see with the "ts" of "Soviets" and "Glints", and the "l" sounds in "steel" and "smile". ASSONANCE, the repetition of similar vowel sounds in close proximity, helps to stress the dualism of Gorbachev being established here with the long "i" vowels in "Behind the smile".

The Metaphors of *Time*

The metaphoric structure of these headings picks up and develops the dualist image of the man of smile and the man of steel. METAPHOR derives from the Greek *metapherein* (*meta*=across; *pherein*=to carry; to carry across). With metaphor we bring a METAPHIER or definer from outside, across to the METAPHAND, which we wish to define. "Steel", as in the phrase "man of steel", has become a cliché through constant use in our language. We have become so habituated to this phrase that we do not stop to recognize the metaphor, in which the metaphier, "steel", defines in a purely linguistic way the metaphand, "man".

metaphier ———————————————————————— metaphand
steel man ———————————————————————— (Gorbachev)

The iron ore of nature transformed through cultural industrial production into steel gets carried over as metaphier to define in less than neutral terms the biological production of nature, the metaphand man, who has presumably been transformed by the Communist Party's industrial reproductive system into Mikhail Gorbachev.

We are so habituated, in naive realist fashion, to spatial metaphors that we usually fail to see signs such as "Behind", in "Behind the smile", that point to a spatial metaphor. In a most literal and truly objective sense, there can be no behind, just as there can be no "sharpness", for "sharpness" is a metaphier brought over from the realm of tools and weapons, just as the metaphier "Glints" comes from the same source. This overall metaphorizing develops intensively the image of dualism, to connect the smiling surface with the "Glints" of a shining, ruthless machine or knife. The inspiration might well be Chaucer (d. 1400), who wrote of "the smiler with the knife under his cloak".

The Metonyms of *Time*

In the headings we meet "the smile", which takes us from metaphor to metonymy. "The smile" is a unit of metonymy. In modern semiotic practice, metonymy and synecdoche tend to become one. METONYMY, a figure of substitution, takes the part of a thing or process to represent the whole thing or process. Metaphor involves two semantic domains and it goes outside the boundaries of the subject under treatment and imports alien metaphiers, but metonymy involves only one semantic domain and stays within its own boundaries to make the part into the whole. Metonymy in this way comes to seem more natural than metaphor, though this is an illusion. As we shall see, problems occur with the one just as easily as with the other, and neither has any claim to absolute truth value. For example, in *TIME*'s own terms, there is more to Gorbachev (the whole) than a smile (the part). Moreover, if we return to the cover text, we will see there the sign sequence, "Moscow's New Boss", where the loaded metaphor "Boss" follows the metonym "Moscow". In this instance, "Moscow" becomes the part which represents the whole of Russia or the USSR. This part has been very carefully chosen by *TIME* to raise all the negative associations of the centre of an internal and external Russian Empire. *TIME* is being somewhat moderate here though because it could have employed the stronger metonym, "The Kremlin".

Visual Metaphors of *Time*

The metaphorizing does not stop with the verbal text. If we go back to the visual images and compare the cover illustration with the one of Gorbachev in the interior text section, we discover that these two faces have very little in common. Yet somehow it is the cover version which seems familiar. The reason for this is that the cover version works metaphorically: Gorbachev's face has been made to look somewhat like that of Chairman Mao because the artist has inserted the visual metaphier Mao under his visual concept or signified of Gorbachev. He has therefore double-signified the portrait visual

13

concept by sliding the Mao metaphier inside or under the Gorbachev portrait concept. By this means, all the key associations regular *TIME* readers would have with Mao get carried over as they look at this portrait: the intelligence, the cunning, the ruthlessness, the inscrutability, and the smile.

The Inner Text of *Time*

We have seen *TIME* constitute Gorbachev in dualist terms, visually and verbally, through the cover portrait and the text, and through the interior headings, but what about the article itself? Here we shall confine ourselves to the opening paragraph to make some necessary points, after making a few comments about the basic literary form *TIME* uses for the article.

The Essay of *Time*

In form, the *TIME* article is an ESSAY. Historically, both the sign "essay" and the form it names come from the French "essai", which became current in English in late sixteenth-century England, at that time very much under the influence of the French sceptical philosopher Michel de Montagne. "Essai" means "an attempt". An attempt at what? An attempt at Truth. It should still be of great concern to us that the late sixteenth century was making attempts at Truth, when we recall the millennia of human experience that had gone before, and more particularly the two thousand years of on-again, off-again theorizing that had come down from classical Greece. Much as in our own day, the late sixteenth century underwent what Thomas Kuhn (in *The Structure of Scientific Revolutions*, 2nd ed.) calls a paradigm shift, a fundamental change in the major presuppositions of current thought. In the sixteenth century, the secular "science" of the new mercantile capitalist order began seriously to replace the theocentric (God-centred) ideology of the old feudal landed classes. Feudalism had constructed an encyclopaedic (though by no means actually consistent or uncontested) vision of reality based on a cosmology which was theocentric. The new age shattered that vision and began to rebuild the edifice of knowledge on secular, scientific foundations. In this process, underdetermined discourse was developed and married to the essay form. Underdetermined discourse thus became the form of discourse automatically associated with Truth—became, in fact, the form of Truth itself.

The Discourse of Truth in *Time*

Like all forms of discourse which have persisted for substantial historical periods, the essay form has been culturally created and socially reproduced.

14

Through historical habituation, however, it has come to seem natural and eternal, a vehicle of The Truth. The proof of this Truth appears to come from the structure of the essay and its seemingly "natural" and "neutral" underdetermined prose. In fact, underdetermined discourse is neither natural nor neutral, as we shall see. Indeed, essays themselves are always artificial constructions, the result of the selection of a number of conventions from a variety of conventions provided by past practice.

The Denotations of *Time*

The first paragraph in the *TIME* essay has seven sentences which, for reasons which will become clear below, we shall arrange visually in the following manner:

	4	
1		5
2		6
3		7

If we wish to the analyze the signs in these sentences to determine whether they are DENOTATIVE (D), and thus have an apparently unemotional mathematical precision, or CONNOTATIVE (C), and thus allow for a variety of subjective and emotional responses, then without question the pattern of this paragraph is consistent:

		4		
1	D	D	5	D
2	D		6	D
3	D		7	D

The paragraph is denotative throughout.

The Deixis of *Time*

This *TIME* essay, like all essays, begins by building and attempting to make credible, or "natural", the world which is its subject. Through the process of DEIXIS (dee-icks-iss), deictic markers or locative devices establish person, time, place, and space. The sequence of third person pronouns "He...He...His..." and the proper name Mikhail Gorbachev establish the textual reality of the new Russian leader. The sequence further sets up an historical time sweep through the past and present verbs "has been described", "is", and "stood", while the powerful deictic "There" places Gorbachev

15

not only under the glare of the TV lights, but at the centre of power in Moscow and on the world stage.

Interest in *Time*

One of the most important things an essay must do is generate and maintain reader interest. Without that it would never be read by its intended audience. One common way of doing this, while simultaneously creating textual cohesion and coherence, is through ANAPHORA (Gk. *ana* = forward, in this context; *pherein* = to carry; to carry forward). In this essay, the repeated third person pronoun ''He'' serves as an anaphoric sequence which generates interest through a touch of mystery and leads up to the dramatic fourth sentence, ''There...stood Mikhail Gorbachev''. The technique is a common one in the discourse of prose fiction.

The Symmetry of *Time*

This fourth spectacular sentence is the centre and pivot on which the first three and last three sentences balance. Some interesting patterns emerge when we look at the paragraph in these terms and begin to discover how data and readers are manipulated. We have already seen that the denotative signs on the level of conceptual meaning are not manipulatory, but that the anaphora is. Here we shall see other evidence of manipulation through structure. In terms of syntax, these seven sentences are either LINEAR (l) subject-verb-object types, or DISLOCATED (d) sentences which relocate elements of the linear sentence into such patterns as the modifier-subject-verb-object sequence. In this paragraph, we find a perfect balance:

		4		
1	l	d	5	d
2	l		6	d
3	l		7	d

A similar balance can be found among the verbs between passive (P) verbs and active (A) verbs:

		4		
1	P	A	5	A
2	P		6	A
3	P		7	A

And so also among the sentences that begin with a third person pronoun (TPP) and those which do not (—):

4 —

1	TPP	5	—
2	TPP	6	—
3	TPP	7	—

These skilful manipulations create the image of Gorbachev in the first three sentences as an enigmatic object who materializes out of nowhere to move onto the centre, public, and world stage under the glare of TV lights. This is largely a result of the formal, denotative, linear sentences in which the third person pronouns initially keep Gorbachev at a distance from the narrator. This distance, reinforced by the deictic "There", also locates the narrator and reader in a relational "here" as spectators to the Gorbachev "There".

The friendly, smiling side of the dualist vision being constituted in *TIME* appears again in the three dislocated sentences which bury the third person pronouns and speak of Gorbachev in his proper name. The friendly smile also gets help here, as we see Gorbachev with his family and joking with reporters. PROXEMICS—the study of spatial relations, desirable and otherwise, between persons and things in different cultures—reveals, in the *TIME* text, an ideological use of space. The great proxemic distance between the joint narrator and reader on the one side here, and Gorbachev over there (these last two commas do the same thing), creates a sense of alienation and mystery in the first four sentences. The near distance of the family and the familiar jokes of the last three sentences makes us recognize Gorbachev as "one of us". The result is a dualist vision.

The Linguistic Codes of *Time*

Thus far we have operated with the classical fiction of the ideal reader, assuming for working purposes that a reader is a reader is a reader. But that is not so. There are levels of competence in reading, and ranges of education and experience distinguish persons and groups of readers from each other. To understand the implications of this for writing in *TIME*, we need to look at Basil Bernstein's London-based study of the social class basis of linguistic codes. Bernstein distinguishes between the elaborated linguistic code of the middle classes and the professions, and the restricted linguistic code of the majority of the working classes. The elaborated linguistic code he refers to is nothing other than the linear, denotative, underdetermined discourse we have already considered, while the restricted linguistic code he refers to resembles syntactically fragmented versions of overdetermined discourse. Since users of the restricted linguistic code frequently have difficulty with the elaborated code and its underdetermined discourse—and big problems with rigorous analysis—it seems likely that the overdetermined headings and cover of *TIME* are aimed at the restricted code of the lower-class audience, while the underdetermined, analytical essays are aimed at the elaborated code of the middle-class audience.

The Morality of *Time*

By combining overdetermined and underdetermined prose in the manner analyzed above, *TIME* has brought back into underdetermined prose discourse, classical rhetoric, "the art of persuasion", which seventeenth-century science sought to banish from underdetermined "plain prose". This development therefore raises the question of the morality of language manipulation, a problem which has bothered moralists and philosophers (even as they used it) for the past two and a half thousand years, beginning with Plato. The essential problem, however, is this: all language usages are manipulative, but in different ways, depending upon their kind and purpose. There is no neutral language or discourse of Truth: there are simply different forms of discourse, employed for different purposes.

The Lessons of *Time*

The lessons of *TIME* are simple, and singular. *TIME* is not immoral in its manipulations. What we have seen is simply *TIME* creating the world in its own ideological image. The question of immorality appears only in the fact that, despite the massive amounts of money spent on teaching language and literature in our society, students are not taught the theory and practice of discourse in our schools. This means that they leave those schools and universities unable to read *TIME* in a proper, intelligent and critical way (and let us now be fair and include *Pravda*, the *Times of London*, *The Globe and Mail*, and so on). That is the lesson of *TIME*, and it is about "time" it is learned.

[The Bracketing of *Time*]

A second lesson (which is actually a corollary to the first) to be learned from *TIME* is applicable to all other texts of all kinds in all disciplines: that we must initially, in our analysis of a text, always read it as a constructed TEXTUAL WORLD distinct from the EMPIRICAL WORLD. Once we see how all texts have been constructed, we can then discover how well the textual world fits the empirical world about which it in some way seeks to speak.

To avoid the naive realist error, then, and to get into the twentieth century before it is too late, we must learn to put the empirical world in brackets [   ]. We must agree not to talk about the empirical world until we understand how the textual world itself works as a text. To learn how the textual world works, we must start with the materiality of language, and to that we now turn.

Semiotics:
Some Basic Definitions and Considerations

Semiotics

SEMIOTICS is the science (L. *scientia* = knowledge) of SIGNS (Gk. *semeion* = a mark) and SIGN SYSTEMS (Gk. *systema* = an organized whole). Our culture consists of a great number of sign systems, large and small. These range from road sign systems, through visual art sign systems, to the sign systems of spoken and written discourse and beyond.

Words, Things, and Reification

Common definition makes nouns stand for things. This attitude easily slides over into the view that words equal the things they are seen to stand for. From there it is easy to take the step to the naive realist assumption that words in some way are the things they stand for. By this means, abstractions deriving from the operations of human thought soon get converted into things. The process of assuming abstractions to be things we call reification, after the Latin word *res* which means "thing". Semiotics avoids this error because of the way in which it defines the sign. Moreover, it uses the term "sign" rather than "word" to escape any naive realist associations that the term "word" may have, though "sign" also has a greater scope of reference than "word".

The Sign

A sign system has as its basic unit the SIGN. The meaning of this extra-ordinarily flexible concept "sign" can only be determined, in a specific instance, by reference to the level on which it is being used. While word and sign on one level may be considered equivalents, sign also can be used to refer to such things as upper-case letters and punctuation marks. On a larger scale of organization, a whole text can be a sign.

Signs, Phonemes, and Graphemes

A spoken language sign consists of one or more PHONEMES (Gk. *phone*=sound) or written equivalents, GRAPHEMES (Gk. *graphein*=to write). Vowels and consonants are phonemes and graphemes. The unobstructed flow of air from the lungs produces phoneme vowels, while manipulated obstructions of various kinds produces a wide range of phoneme consonants. The written form of the graphemes is a second order sign system. English has more phonemes than graphemes, with the result that some graphemes have to represent a range of phonemes. For example, the "a" in "far", "fat", and "fate".

Phonemes, Graphemes, and Syllables

The phoneme/grapheme units make up syllables, which may be single vowels, as in the indefinite article "a" below, or a combination of consonants and vowel as in "a man ran" below:

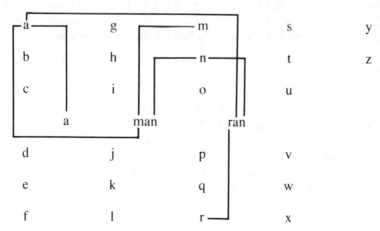

Syllables ending on a vowel we call open syllables, while those ending on

21

consonants we call closed, though near vowels such as the "r" in "far" have the open quality.

Syllables, Signs, and Morphemes

Signs may be single syllables, as above, or multiples up to the size of "antidisestablishmentarianism". Single or multi-syllable signs may be viewed as MORPHEMES (Gk. *morphos*=shape), and morphemes may be free and unbound, or bound. The signs "fond" and "fondly" differ by virtue of the addition of the suffix "ly" (L. *suffixus*=to fasten on beneath). "Fond" works as a free morpheme because it can stand by itself in a sentence, while "ly" must be bound to a free or unbound morpheme. The prefix "un" in unbound cannot stand by itself, but "bound" can.

The Binary Character of Signs

Binary in structure (L. *binarius*=in two parts), the sign consists of a SIGNIFIER and a SIGNIFIED. Signifier refers to the material phonemes or graphemes as in d-o-g, in isolation from any conceptual meaning. Signified refers to the mental concept attached by convention to the material signifier. This signified "dog" is not Fido the family dog, but a high level abstraction.

The Arbitrariness of Signifiers

No necessary connection, only convention, joins the material signifier to the mentally and socially signified concept. Were there a direct and "natural" connection between the two, we would find only one language in the world. Language is therefore not "natural", but an invention of culture.

The Slipperiness of Signifieds

In the course of history a signified may slip out from under a signifier: our sign "nice" meant foolish in the Middle Ages, and "democracy" had strong negative meanings until around 1780 when social changes began to push the old signified out from under the signifier in favour of more positive meanings. In very recent times we have seen the sign "gay" appropriated, which is to say re-signified, by homosexuals.

Sign and Significatum

We define SIGNIFICATUM as the "object" to which a sign refers. We use "object" here in the philosophical sense: "object" may be a thing or a concept, it may be in the empirical world or inside language.

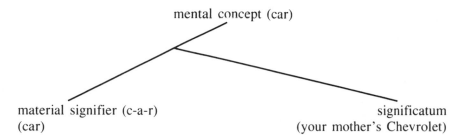

mental concept (car)

material signifier (c-a-r)   significatum
(car)   (your mother's Chevrolet)

Transitive, Intransitive Signs

The car example above is a TRANSITIVE SIGN with its referent significatum a concrete object in the empirical world. An INTRANSITIVE SIGN refers inwards to the processes of thought and language, and includes signs such as "and", "if", and "but", none of which can be found in car showrooms, on the streets, or growing on trees.

Constituting the Object

The naive realist view presupposes that words/names equal things, and that some essential connection or affinity joins words and things "naturally" in a way that allows nature to be brought over into culture. In fact, the process of naming does not grasp the totality of anything, but simply determines how the referent significatum will be seen. The naming thus constitutes the object. Changed times and changed ways of seeing will produce other kinds of naming and constituting of the "same" object.

Semiosis

Signs do not usually work by themselves but in sequences fused together by SEMIOSIS. In the process of becoming an example of DIEGESIS (Gk. *diegesis* = narration), or MIMESIS (Gk. *mimesis* = representation of empirical reality), a text will always create a semiosis, and it must be examined as such. The relationship between a textual world and the empirical world is not an IMMEDIATE one but is always MEDIATED. To avoid confusion when analyzing a text, we must therefore remember that—as Michael Rifaterre is so fond of saying— before diegesis, and before mimesis, comes semiosis.

Syntactics

SYNTACTICS refers to the uses to which syntax may be put. SYNTAX, derived from the Greek *syntaxis*, an arrangement, has to do with the ways in which we order signs into sequences to suit the purposes of our discourse. Taking into account the needs of all the forms of discourse, we necessarily find a variety of orders. We cannot say that there is some natural or right way of ordering signs in general, because the right way can only be suited to the needs of the particular kind of discourse. What is right for a scientific essay will often in some sense be wrong for the needs of poetic discourse or the discourse of prose fiction, and so on.

Since there are no privileged forms of discourse, but rather only different forms of discourse used for different purposes, there can be no privileging of a particular way of ordering signs. How, then, do we generate a particular sentence which we can use as a standard for descriptive purposes? We agree for heuristic purposes (Gk. *heuriri* = to invent) to invent a model from existing practice without committing ourselves to the view that this "normative" sentence is normal and that other forms are abnormal.

We here select, for heuristic purposes, the linear subject-verb-object sequence (since, in our culture, this form of syntax is the one which most closely approximates in form the structure of what we think of as Truth).

Normative Linear Syntax

For present purposes we shall rearrange the first sentence from Sinclair Ross' short story, "The Lamp At Noon" ("A little before noon she lit the lamp"), to turn it into a normative linear syntactical arrangement, thus:

She lit the lamp a little before noon.

Here the subject ("she") precedes the verb ("lit") and the object of the subject's verb/action ("the lamp"), itself followed by the time qualifier, "a little before noon".

The linear quality of this normative syntax we term the SYNTAGMA. We say it is SYNTAGMATIC. This syntagmatic "style" commonly gives expression to linear or superpositional thought (see p. 104), and it may be used to create either underdetermined or overdetermined discourse (see p. 10). The modified Ross sentence here is syntagmatic while also being over-determined, as the functional alliteration and assonance indicate (see pp. 106-7).

Dislocated Syntax

Dislocated syntax relocates one or more of the elements of a normative (not normal) sentence, as we can see in the original version of Ross' first sentence:

A little before noon she lit the lamp.

In the original version, the time qualifier "A little before noon" has been moved from the end of the normative version, to the beginning of the dislocated version.

Fragmented Syntax

Fragments are of two basic kinds: intentional and unintentional. The unintentional will almost invariably be problematical because it unintentionally leaves out elements of the normative or dislocated orders, and these forms will therefore now not make sense, or will make the wrong kind of sense. Intentional fragments generally do not belong—or are not allowed—in the highly formal discourse of prose non-fiction, but can work—and are allowed—in less formal non-fiction. Certainly intentional fragments have a place in prose fiction and in the discourse of poetry. We can use the same example to make the point:

She lit the lamp. A little before noon.

This latter fragment has deliberately dropped the subject and the verb, though

26

it relies on the CONTEXT of the subject-verb-object sequence which precedes it.

Simple and Elaborate Sequences

Syntactical orders may be simple sentences, or elaborated compound and complex sentences. They may be normative, dislocated, fragmented, or combinations of these. "She lit the lamp" is a simple sequence, while the one that follows it in the Ross text is not.

> Demented wind fled keening past the house:
> a wail through the eaves that died every minute or two.

Demented wind drops the DETERMINER (so-called because here it would determine that a noun will follow), the definite article "the", while "a wail in the eaves" has no subject or verb. The fragmentation of the syntax acts out the fragmentation of the textual reality that the sign sequence signifies.

Ellipsis

Ellipsis derives from the Greek *elleipein*, which means omission. In grammar, this means the omission of a sign which the reader understands from the context, even in its absence. Ellipsis invites reader participation to fill in the gaps.

Why Syntactical Variety?

Why the range of syntactical possibilities? Technically it would be possible to have an endless string of subject-verb-object linear sequences of signs, but a heavy price would have to be paid for such practice:

a) such linearity would be predictable and hence boring;

b) it would reduce the rich multiplicity of discourse forms to essentially one;

c) it would prevent the expression of complex shadings of thought and feeling;

d) it would therefore reduce our ability to understand ourselves and our environment from other important angles of written discourse.

Semantics

Semantics is the science (L. *scientia* = knowledge) of meaning in a context where "meaning" refers to the significance of concepts: conceptual meaning. In fact, independent of the conceptual meaning of signifieds in a sequence of signs, sequences of material signifiers themselves generate meaning, as we shall see.

The Semantics of Conceptual Meaning; Positive and Negative

Ferdinand de Saussure, founder of modern linguistic and semiotic studies, opposed the notion of positive definitions of the conceptual meaning of signs with the idea of definition by negation. We find an example of positive definition in the familiar sign sequence "a tree is X". Such definitions set up the conditions which allow naive realism to confuse the very high level abstraction which is the sign "tree", with significata "trees" in the forests of nature and the gardens of culture. Negative definition refers to the distinction between the very abstract concept "tree" inside the language system, and all the other signifieds in that system. This way of proceeding very correctly establishes the sign system as a functional whole in relation to, but distinct from, the empirical world. Whereas looking at a sign as an individual rather than as part of a system leads to the naive realist fusion of the sign with its object, seeing signs as a system constantly reminds us that:

a) language "constitutes" the empirical world, causes us to see it in a particular way;

b) signified concepts inside the language system can remain unchanged while our understanding of empirical reality does change.

Thus, the naive realist concepts constituted by the sign sequence "the sun rises" still live a vital existence in most vocabularies, hundreds of years after the Ptolemaic cosmological system, to which this notion belonged, has been refuted.

The Semantics of Syntax

The semantics of syntax has to do with the ways in which the manipulation of signs may have profound effects on the meaning of a sign sequence. If we look again at the opening, actual, dislocated sentence from "The Lamp at Noon", along with its revised linear version, we shall discover one of the possibilities for a change in meaning through syntactical variation:

> linear: She lit the lamp a little before noon.
> dislocated: A little before noon she lit the lamp.

The linear version FOREGROUNDS the "She" against the BACK-GROUND of the action "lit", the object "lamp" and the time "a little before noon". In general, this order suggests a "She" (and note the fore-grounding capital or upper case letter) who dominates events. By contrast, the dislocated version places the backgrounding, lower case "she", amidst other backgrounding time and events to suggest someone much less in command of events. This exactly matches the situation in which we find this woman in the larger text: overwhelmed by a crying baby; by a howling wind; by a drought on the farm; by economic poverty; and by a dominating patriarchal husband. The dislocated syntactical order thus makes this first sentence a genuine microcosm of the macrocosmic text as a whole, whereas the linear version would have suggested her control over events, an attitude which would contradict all but the last few lines of the macrocosmic text.

It is worth looking at several more examples of the semantics of sign order at this point.

The initial lines of "Strike", by Canada's first avant-garde painter, Bertram Brooker, use two different syntactical orders to denote two different human states:

She sits there
Fiddling with the greasy table cloth
George
Strike
Whisky
Thirteen weeks
And now a general strike

The first two lines constitute a single linear sentence. This creates for us, through the eyes of a narrator, an outwardly unified and substantial person: this woman. The conventionally unified linear sentence thus comes to constitute, and therefore represent, the conventionally unified, physical, surface person, which itself stands for the classical nineteenth-century bourgeois ego, the person with a proper name. But outward physical unity can be an appearance which masks inner turmoil and psychological fragmentation. Brooker captures this twentieth-century inner state for us by making his transcendental (beyond experience) narrator disappear, along with the normative and objective linear sentence, and by moving to the immanental (within things), inner fragmented state represented by the syntax fragments which follow. The poem as a whole makes clear that the fragmented inner, subjective condition, and the outer fragmented, objective socio-economic condition of industrial strife, are but two sides of the same coin.

In his *On the Constitution of the Church and State*, Samuel Taylor Coleridge employs a similar semantically charged opposition of syntax. He speaks for himself and his own side of the argument in a carefully balanced underdetermined prose non-fiction to create an overwhelming sense of sweet reason for his position: "That which contemplated objectively (i.e. as existing externally to the mind) we call a LAW; the same contemplated subjectively (i.e. as existing in a subject or mind) is an idea". And again: "By an idea, I mean (in this instance) that conception of a thing, in which the thing may happen to exist at this or at that time; nor yet generalized from any number or succession of such forms or modes; but which is given by the knowledge of its ultimate aim". Such, then, is the voice of the sweet reason of underdetermined prose, the writer's argument. Next we meet the enemy, those without reason, the "anarchists", who are represented by verbless syntax fragments of overdetermined prose: "Talents without genius; a swarm of clever, well-informed men; an anarchy of minds, a despotism of maxims. Despotism in government and legislation—of vanity and sciolism in the intercourse of life—of presumption, temerity and hardness of heart, in political economy". And yet again: "Government by journeymen clubs; by saint and sinner societies; committees, institutions, by reviews, magazines, and above all by newspapers".

It will be obvious by now that syntax has semantic significance, and that meaning can be manipulated from within the material signifier system, a system which conventional language theory takes to be neutral.

The Semantics of Phonemes

The semantics of phonemes refers to the way in which the repetition of phonemes in reasonable proximity to each other will link signs which contain repeated sounds. This process foregrounds the complete signs to which the repeated phonemes are attached and distinguishes them from other signs in a sequence to give them emphasis. Having done their regular work in a sequence, repeated sounds give the signs of which they are a part a second chance through emphatic foregrounding. This happens in the same first sentence by Sinclair Ross, where we find an example of alliteration, the repetition of initial consonant sounds in close proximity to each other:

A little before noon she lit the lamp.

This sequence repeats the "l" phoneme to join "little", "lit", and "lamp".

The same sentence also has assonance, the repetition of similar vowel sounds in close proximity to each other. We find an example with the short "i" phoneme in "little" and "lit" (and, in some pronunciations, the "e" in the first syllable of "before"). The repeated sounds must be in close proximity because sight and sound organs have an extremely short SENSORY MEMORY (in the rods and cones of the eye and holding mechanism in the ear) which puts sights and sounds onto a short hold until perception decides what to dismiss and what to send on to the next stage, the short term memory system itself. A repeated sight or sound within close temporal proximity will retrieve its predecessor before it has time to decay or go into short term memory. This allows repeated sounds both to destroy the space and time that separate them, and to foreground the signs to which they are attached against the background of the line in which they are imbedded.

The Semantics of Figuration

Underdetermined discourse emphasizes the signifieds, the semantics of conceptual meaning, and seeks to suppress the material signifier system as an element of meaning, the semantics of formal (structural) meaning. To do that, underdetermined discourse will in its most formal usages (in the spirit of The Royal Society) seek to avoid the active use of METAPHOR (see p. 41). It will employ DEAD METAPHOR freely enough, because that kind of metaphor has become dead to narrow rational consciousness through habituation, but underdetermined discourse has been traditionally suspicious of LIVE METAPHOR. Underdetermined discourse aspires to a condition of logic, mathematical precision, and for this reason metaphor becomes an embarrassment to it. To use metaphor means admitting that mathematical precision in language cannot be achieved.

The Semantics of Sentence Mood

Sign sequences that make up sentences may be declarative, interrogative, imperative or exclamatory. What they are may be signified by the syntactical order of the sentence (and thus included in semantics of syntax above), as with the imperative in Donne's "Holy Sonnet" (Sonnet 7):

> At the round earth's imagined corners, *blow*
> Your trumpets, angels, and *arise, arise*
> From death, you numberless infinities
> Of souls, and to your scattered bodies *go*.   [italics mine]

Or the exclamatory, interrogative, and declarative sequence in Marlowe's *Doctor Faustus* (**IV**, iv):

> Martino: What ho, Benvolio!
> Benvolio: Here, what, Frederick, ho!
> Frederick: O help me, gentle friend; where is Martino?
> Martino: Dear Frederick, here,
>   Half smothered in a lake of mud and dirt,
>   Through which the furies dragged me by the heels.

In this sequence, the exclamation mark is a material sign which signifies the concept "this is an exclamation", while the question mark signifies "question", and the period at the end of Martino's sequence says "I am probably declarative", a probability which is confirmed by scrutiny of the sequence itself.

The proportion of each of these sentences to a part of a text, or in relation to the whole of the text, can itself shift the conceptual meaning of the part or the whole. For example, the underdetermined discourse of prose non-fiction may begin with an implicit or explicit question but it will typically consist of declarative sentences which seek to "declare" the truth of a subject.

The Semantics of Rhythm

This subject will be dealt with more fully below, but for the moment we may briefly distinguish between METRE (Gk. *metron*), and RHYTHM (Gk.

rhythmos). Metre is a mental concept of quantified perfection abstracted from the material practice of rhythm. Metre is the perfected mental notion of the rhythm of the empirical world:

$$\frac{\text{Metre}}{\text{Rhythm}}$$

If we take the iambic rhythm with its soft/loud (∪ /) IAMBUS as a basic unit, we immediately note that in practice no two of these rhythmic units are ever exactly alike. In our mental category of the iambic metre, however, every iambus is exactly the same. This means that, once we have learned the rhythmic codes, we will be aware of a constant, shifting tension between the quantified perfection of the metre in the mind, and the "imperfect" form it takes as a material rhythm in the empirical world.

The opening of Shakespeare's "Sonnet 12" has an undisturbed iambic rhythm:

∪ / ∪ / ∪ / ∪ / ∪ /
When I / do count / the clock / that tells / the time

However, the second line disturbs this pattern:

∪ / ∪ / / / ∪ / ∪ /
And see / the brave / day sunk / in hid / eous night

This line basically continues the iambic rhythm to establish the iambic as the normative rhythm for this discourse. However, it also introduces a SPONDEE (loud/loud; / /) into the third foot (unit of rhythm) to cause a variation. Whereas with the semantics of phonemes we saw a variety of different phonemes forming the background for the foregrounded repeated phonemes, here, with rhythm, we have the reverse structure. But the effect is just the same. The foregrounded spondee gives "day sunk" great emphasis. Since the signs in the first line (because of the alliteration, assonance and rhythm together) tick like a clock, this disruption through rhythmic variation allows the organic and qualitative order of nature to disrupt the mechanical order of quantitative clock time (culture), a process made all the more effective by virtue of the fact that "sunk" is a nautical (the sea: nature) metaphor of disaster. Rhythmic variation thus creates powerful semantic meaning.

The Semantics of Juncture

This subject will also be dealt with below, but we may quickly see how

JUNCTURE (pauses) produces semantic meaning in a few lines of poetry. In Donne's "The Canonization", the technique of juncture sets up dualist patterns:

> With wealth your state // your mind with arts improve
> Take you a course // get you a place
> Observe his honour // or his grace
> Or the king's real // or his stamped face

Juncture can also create multiple part line structures where (in the example below) the four-part structure of the material base supports the four-part conceptual meaning of the seasonal year referred to by the sequence of signifieds. This we find in Donne's "The Good-Morrow":

> Love // all alike // no season knows // nor clime
> Nor hours // days // months // which are the rags of time

In Yeats' "The Second Coming", we see that the semicolon juncture cannot hold against the pull of the sentence:

> Things fall apart; the centre cannot hold

The Semantics of Pitch

Together with rhythm, stress, and juncture, PITCH makes up the intonational patterns of a sentence. We can readily see how pitch can change meaning with simple examples:

rising pitch: really   well   no

falling pitch: really   well   no

All of these semantic manipulations of elements on the plane of expression are common to overdetermined discourse, and they distinguish that discourse from underdetermined discourse, a discourse which seeks to repress the material plane of expression (finally in vain).

Pragmatics

PRAGMATICS may be defined as the study of the relationships between the writer, the text, and the reader, or rather readers, since there is no ideal, single kind of reader.

Text

The sign "text" comes from the Latin *textus* meaning "woven", as in fabrics. The term thus draws attention to the constructed character of literary and other texts. A text may be a single sentence or a long novel, but whatever the length, it will have about it a sense of completeness. Thus, "The dog walked down the street" is not a text, while "A stitch in time saves nine" is, along with the novel *War and Peace* and other such works.

Poem

"Poem" derives from the Greek *poema*, which means "the thing made". "Poet", from the Greek *poetes*, means "a maker". All literary texts—indeed, all texts—must be made, and all literary texts must be made by makers, so in this sense all literary writers must be poets. In practice, however, "poet" refers to the maker of poetic discourse.

Reader/Listener/Narrattee

The poet or literary author writes or speaks to a reader, listener, or narrattee. Both the narrator and that reader, listener, or narrattee must in some sense be inside the written or spoken text. Otherwise there could be no communication.

Codes

Society has a SOCIOLECT, a widely available social store of lore and knowledge. From this sociolect the writer draws much of his data. Through the use of different levels of this sociolect, the writer can be sure of making contact with the audience or audiences aimed at. Additionally, there will be the IDIOLECT. This idiolect refers to the store of subjective experience of the writer. Some of this idiolect may become part of the sociolect, but only after it has been published in discourse form.

The sociolect includes a wide variety of CODES (L. *codex*). These codes range from food codes, to dress, footwear, hair styles, furnishings, architectural, linguistic, political, economic, social, artistic codes, and so on.

Weltanschauung

WELTANSCHAUUNG, borrowed directly from German, refers to the world vision of the maker of literary (or other) texts. The kind of values affirmed or disaffirmed in a text will indicate the writer's vision of the world (always bearing in mind that things may not be what they appear to be, as in ironic texts).

The Non-Neutrality of Language

In *Poetry As Discourse*, Antony Easthope argues that language is not a natural, neutral and transparent medium; is not objective. Language is not like a telephone wire (which, in fact, also prevents "clear" communication) in which a sender is said to send a message down to a receiver. First of all, the sender is not an isolated, independent, objective being who can get outside of language, and yet still communicate through language. And neither can the receiver stand outside of the way in which he has been inscribed, written into, by language. The individual, then, can never get outside of language. Moreover, culture, not nature, produces language, the sounds of language themselves being a cultural selection from the range of potential noises nature makes possible.

Hearing and Overhearing

The alien quality we feel in works from the past arises out of the difference between our sociolect in the present and the sociolect which informed the text in the past. A reader in the past would feel at home with the text in the past because its values in some way approximated his own, or at least belonged to his time and so he was familiar with them. That past reader heard the text clearly because he understood the codes that structure its sociolect. We, however, overhear the text through the filters of our different but related sociolect.

The Communication Chain

author outside text	author or narrative persona inside text	text context codes	listener or narrattee inside text	reader outside text

"Persona" descends from the Latin *personare*, which meant "to sound through". It refers to the masks worn by actors on the Roman stage, through which they spoke. These actors thus adopted a role, but not one whose values the actor necessarily shared. And so the narrator (L. *narrare*=to relate, make known) does not necessarily represent the views of the writer. In "A Modest Proposal" by Jonathan Swift, for example, the narrator advocates the eating of human babies, but the author intends rather to save human babies from misery, not to eat them.

Narrators have been called RELIABLE or UNRELIABLE, which is to say that they can be trusted or not be trusted. This becomes a complex problem in changing times such as the present when a narrator accepted as reliable in past texts now becomes the object of scrutiny, since he proves to be by no means neutral in his views. There can thus be different degrees of agreement and disagreement between a writer and a persona or narrator, and those degrees can change over time.

Thematics

We may define THEMATICS in two related ways:

a)   the way in which a writer gives his theme or themes shape in the discourse language of a text so as to thematize his problematic (Gk. *problema*, Fr. *problematique*, a difficult problem posed);

b)   the study of the way in which a writer gives his theme or themes shape as he thematizes his problematic.

   The process of thematization varies with the different forms of discourse.
   Shakespeare's "Sonnet 73" and T.S. Eliot's "The Love Song of J. Alfred Prufrock" both thematize the problematic of the self-conscious ego ("I"): the Shakespeare poem at the beginning of bourgeois individualism (the beginning of the more or less solid "I"); and the Prufrock text at the end of this period, when the "I" has reached the point of fragmentation and disintegration in the Age of Freud. Both poems represent their times because their conception of the "I" gives expression to the dominant tendencies of their times.

Thematization of the I: "Sonnet 73"

> That time of year thou mayst in me behold
> When yellow leaves, or none, or few, do hang

Upon those boughs which shake against the cold
Bare ruined choirs where late the sweet birds sang.
In me thou seest the twilight of such day
As after sunset fadeth in the west,
Which by and by black night doth take away,
Death's second self that seals up all in rest:
In me thou seest the glowing of such fire
That on the ashes of his youth doth lie
As the death bed whereon it must expire,
Consumed with that which it was nourished by:
 This thou perceivest, which makes thy love more strong
 To love that well which thou must leave ere long.

The insistent and anaphoric "in me" (lines 1, 5, 9) creates a powerful sense of the new, integrated, unified bourgeois "I". The firm individual speaking voice appears through superpositional thought (in which concept follows concept in uninterrupted linear fashion—see p. 104) and syntagmatic sentences bound together globally by the anaphora. This strong "I" at the beginnings of bourgeois individualism becomes aware of its isolated and vulnerable state because it must die. Corporate individualism of the feudal period knew all about death, but did not respond to it in quite the same individual way because the individual was not isolated in society. This isolation came with the increasing possessive individualism of Shakespeare's day, as revealed in his text.

Thematization of the I: "The Love Song of J. Alfred Prufrock"

We can get some sense of what the much longer poem by Eliot is about if we look at the first fourteen lines:

Let us go then, you and I,
When the evening is spread out against the sky
Like a patient etherised upon a table;
Let us go, through certain half deserted streets,
The muttering retreats
Of restless nights in one-night cheap hotels
·And sawdust restaurants with oyster shells:
Streets that follow like a tedious argument
Of insidious intent
To lead you to an overwhelming question...
Oh, do not ask,"What is it?"
Let us go and make our visit.

> In the room the women come and go
> Talking of Michelangelo.

Eliot creates a sense of the fragmentation of the ego and the modern age through the fragmentation of textual poetic form. Indeed, he presupposes the tight syntagmatic style, superpositional thought and solid ego of the Shakespeare textual world, against the background of which his fragmented textual world of Prufrock makes sense. The cohesion and coherence and the superpositional thought of the Shakespeare text appear in the first twelve lines of the Eliot text, but give way to a gap which breaks cohesion and coherence between lines 12 and 13. This introduces—in the manner of film—juxtapositional thought which juxtaposes lines 13 and 14 alongside the first twelve. The irregular line lengths and breaks in rhyme, which fragment the old poetic textual order, also help to create the sense of disintegration.

The language of love is the language of "we", not the language of "I", yet Prufrock contains nearly forty instances of the pronoun "I", almost one for every three lines. The pronoun "we" does not appear until close to the end of the poem, and even there the "we" suggests the royal "we", a disguised "I". The poem has a mere sprinkling of plural "us" pronouns and second person "you" pronouns, but we never learn who the "you" is. Community, hence love, is absent from this poem, which explains the irony of the text.

From Shakespeare to Eliot

If community has fragmented to produce the narcissistic "I" which is Prufrock, in the same process it has fragmented that ego. The poem dramatizes the "slipping" of the signified old bourgeois ego (the early textual version of which was Shakespeare's speaker) from under the signifier "I". Eliot resignifies that ego in much the same way as Freud resignified the solid old bourgeois ego into divided and warring parts, and in just the same way as the physicists resignified the solid, indivisible atom (Gk. *atomos*=indivisible) as splittable in the twentieth century.

Both these texts therefore thematize the problematic of the "I" at different points in time, the Shakespeare poem thematizing the new, isolated but solid "I", aware of its isolation, and the Eliot poem the modern, alienated "I", aware of its isolation and disintegration under modern urban conditions.

Metaphor

The sign "metaphor" has its origins in the Greek *metapherein* (*meta*=across; *pherein*=to carry) and means "to carry across". It involves two semantic domains and requires two distinct, yet in some way similar, "objects" (philosophically not necessarily "things"), the one of which is carried over to define, alter, colour, or modify the other. This can happen in music, and it regularly happens in jazz, or in visual art, as we saw earlier with the Mao/Gorbachev portrait (p. 13), or it can happen in everyday and literary (spoken and written) language. Metaphor, then, requires a target object to be identified, and another object which reshapes the target object by being carried over to it. The target object we call the METAPHAND, while the object carried over to do the defining, altering, colouring, or modifying, we call the METAPHIER.

Types of Metaphor

Naive Realism and "Dead" Metaphor

Naive realism, through habituation to language, confuses nature with cultural creations by assuming certain metaphors to be natural, which means that they are not recognized as metaphors at all. For the naive realist, the sun really does "rise" in the morning. These metaphors-not-perceived-of-as-metaphors we commonly call DEAD METAPHORS. But take this very phrase "dead

41

metaphors'': it is itself a metaphor, where we watch the metaphier "death" being "carried across" from organic life, to define the target object (an abstract concept) or metaphand in language. The dead metaphor "the sun rises" proves to be a "common sense" remnant of the old pre-Renaissance Ptolemaic cosmology, one which assumed a static earth at the centre of the universe around which all heavenly bodies revolved.

It seems fairly clear that "dead" metaphors become dead only by habituation of consciousness, but live a very active life (note the metaphor; we cannot escape them) in the unconscious levels of the mind, "in" the very structures of consciousness. A metaphor therefore will be dead to consciousness if we have learned to let it slip through the screens of our consciousness without drawing attention to itself. By doing that, by "recognizing" itself in our unconscious, it thus circularly perpetuates the naive realist's way of looking at the world: "behind our backs", so to speak.

Dead metaphors constantly re-inscribe us with the basic mechanism of naive realism. This explains why, on certain levels, both educated and uneducated individuals can share the same erroneous views. Referring to the process of social inscription and reproduction, and to the habituation to received ideas that blinds us to these inscriptions and reproductions, Lakoff and Johnson in *Metaphors We Live By* correctly observe that "our conceptual system is not something we are aware of. In most of the little things we do every day we simply think and act more or less automatically along certain [prescribed] lines.''

Lakoff and Johnson note the mutually supporting function of structural metaphors. Since these deep and hidden metaphors form part of a system, we must deal with them not in isolation from each other, as in common practice, but as part of a system or sub-system, a set. Thus, these writers take the conceptual metaphor "argument is war" and offer a number of examples:

> Your argument is indefensible.
> He attacked every weak point in the argument.
> His criticisms were right on target.
> I demolished his argument.

The deep-rootedness of the "argument is war" attitude signifies the fundamentally aggressive and belligerent attitude of our culture, no matter what other pretty illusions we may have about our culture. These military metaphors, in fact, pervade the whole of our society (where we read of the "fight" to save the seals, the "battle" against cancer, etc.).

One by one Lakoff and Johnson work their way through five sub-systems of culturally created metaphors which, through habituation, we commonly take as real, and which serve as the foundation for the naive realist way of perceiving the world: spatial metaphors, orientational metaphors, conduit metaphors, journey metaphors, and metaphors of time. These five systems of metaphor reveal our fundamental and erroneous sense of space: we see "ups" and "downs" (he's feeling up/down, the stock market's up/down) when there is no literal up or down; we hear that "the bank came across", when there is no literal across; we are told the country "came through its crisis" when there is no journey and no coming through; we read that "he's in trouble" when there can be no "in"; and we say "in front of that tree" when the tree has no literal front. We find time treated the same way when we read of "being in time", "being on time", and "time is money", when time is not money, and we are neither in nor on time.

As CONSCIOUS METAPHORS, all these signs allow for a remarkable economy of language which can "save time", but, when taken literally to be eternal facts of nature, to be natural, they smuggle what is called a "naive realist" set of assumptions into our structures of perception, a set of assumptions that have no bearing whatsoever on an objective empirical world. This practice becomes the basis for a thoroughly erroneous "common sense" view of the world which is only "common sense" because we all agreed, so long ago now that we have forgotten about it, to arbitrarily see the objective, empirical world in that way. We call this view of the world "naive realist" because people who share this view have forgotten that it took millennia of common, cultural effort to draw up the very sophisticated set of metaphors which arbitrarily delineate the axioms of perception (the filters) through which we talk about what is "real".

Mixed Metaphor

Mixed metaphor is a different matter. We find two basic views on mixed metaphor in critical literature: one approving, the other disapproving. Mixed metaphors require some skill to do well, as Shakespeare demonstrated so often, and they demand constant vigilance if we are to avoid creating them unconsciously ourselves. Generally, unconscious mixed metaphors must be avoided, for they can be an embarrassment. Here is an embarrassing one: in the midst of heated partisan debate, a British Councillor said vehemently of his opponent: "He's trying to bulldoze it through with soft soap".

We have here:

a) .He is trying to bulldoze (bulldozer=metaphier) it (metaphand=the process of passing the bill) through.

b) He is trying to soft soap (soft soap=metaphier) it (metaphand=the process of passing the bill) through. (We should note that hard soap used to be diluted to make a lubricant in order to ease the insertion of tight bushings into their metal cases. What was tight and difficult became easy through soft soap. By metaphorical transfer, this process came to define the smooth, oily salesman or politician who could ease his way into or out of any tight situation).

Clearly a heavy metal bulldozer makes sense, and the soft soap metaphor makes sense, but a bulldozer made of soft soap produces an occasion for laughter.

Mixed and Dead Metaphor

More often than not, bad mixed metaphors arise out of the unconscious use of dead metaphor in an inappropriate context. Here are two examples:

a) The leader of a Canadian political party found himself and his leadership challenged, with a party convention imminent. Asked if he would attend, he replied in unconsciously classical style: "If I'm going to be stabbed in the back, I'm going to be there". The problem here arises from his failure to discern "stab in the back" as a metaphier, drawn from literal murder, to define the metaphand, the political treachery aimed at removing him from office.

b) Another classic is the statement that "a verbal agreement is not worth the paper it is written on".

Metaphor in Context

Metaphor and Shakespeare's "Sonnet 73"

That time of year thou mayst in me behold
When yellow leaves, or none, or few, do hang
Upon those boughs which shake against the cold,
Bare ruined choirs where late the sweet birds sang:
In me thou seest the twilight of such day
As after sunset fadeth in the west,
Which by and by black night doth take away,
Death's second self that seals up all in rest.
In me thou seest the glowing of such fire
That on the ashes of his youth doth lie
As the death-bed whereon it must expire,
Consumed with that which it was nourished by:
   This thou perceivest, which makes thy love more strong
   To love that well which thou must leave ere long.

In terms of its rhyme structure, these fourteen lines divide into three quatrains (four-line units) with a rhyme scheme of abab (behold, hang, cold, sang), cdcd (day, west, away, rest,), efef (fire, lie, expire, by), and a rhyming couplet gg (strong, long).

A different cyclical metaphor dominates each of these quatrains, and these unfold in a descending order of magnitude.

THE CYCLES
(metaphiers)

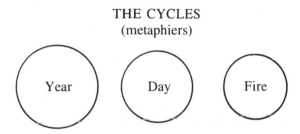

The first quatrain introduces the cycle of the seasons as a metaphier to define the metaphand, human life:

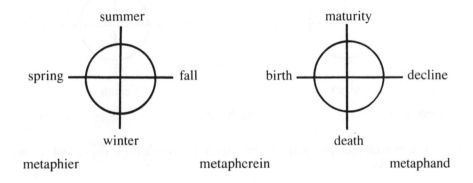

The metaphor takes the four-part metaphier and carries it across to define the related four-part metaphand (bearing in mind that the four-part structures are themselves cultural constructs or explanations, not facts of nature).

The second quatrain repeats this comparison of two four-part cycles, but on a smaller order of magnitude than the first:

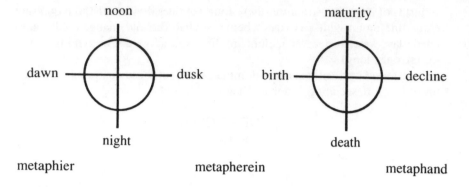

metaphier   metapherein   metaphand

The third quatrain continues the reduction:

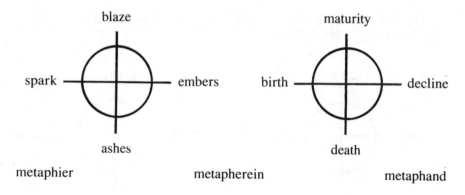

metaphier   metapherein   metaphand

The overall metaphorical pattern which emerges can be expressed in the following way:

But this does not end the subject of metaphor in "Sonnet 73". Not only does this poem carry over metaphiers from the realm of nature to define human life, but it reverses the process to define nature in human or anthropomorphic terms.

PERSONIFICATION (L. *persona*) or ANTHROPOMORPHIZATION (Gk. *anthropos*=person; *morphos*=shape) is a form of metaphor in which a metaphier from the human or animal organic realm gets carried over to a metaphand in non-organic nature so as to define it. This gives to the metaphand some organic, which is to say living, qualities. The signs "hang" and "shake" and "sweet birds sang" do this in the first quatrain. Certainly "hang" works metaphorically to suggest, through the metaphier of judicial hanging (by the neck until dead—and even drawing and quartering in those days), that the leaves have been sentenced to death. Certainly also the leaves, through the metaphier of "shake", are given the human quality of shivering in this cold season. Meanwhile, the "sweet birds sang" refers to the recently migrated birds, and "sweet" is a mixed metaphier carried over for purposes of definition. Meanwhile, these literal birds become simultaneously a metaphier whose metaphand is the long deceased choirboys who used to sing in this ruined church (probably abandoned after the nationalization of the Church by Henry VIII).

Personification proceeds through "black night doth take away" and "Death's second self", shifting to a different metaphier with "seals" and "rest" (the latter also a EUPHEMISM, a figure of substitution which avoids distasteful signs and thoughts by substituting less problematical ones, here "rest" for "death").

By dealing with man through metaphiers drawn from nature, and nature with metaphiers drawn from the human realm, Shakespeare presents humans as being involved in the processes of nature. This is of cultural significance because this kind of picture of humans in nature, and nature in humans, belongs to the period just before the scientific revolution and the separation of humans from nature, a separation made on the assumption that the human could be an objective observer of nature. That view has come to grief in our own time. Ruskin in the late nineteenth century would speak of "the pathetic fallacy", the practice of anthropomorphizing nature. But he was on the other side of the seventeenth-century separation, while Shakespeare was just before and on the edge of it. He could therefore not be accused of indulging in a "pathetic fallacy".

Overdetermined Metaphor

Quite apart from the question of mixed metaphors, some metaphors have more than one dimension. It therefore becomes important, in the process of analyzing metaphor, to ensure that, after we have completed our initial survey of the elements of a metaphor, we do not leave anything behind. This kind of omission often happens in discussions of the "no man is an island" metaphor of the older John Donne (d. 1632). Donne's statement is part of a negation of the developing view of the new bourgeois individualism: a view that "every man is an island'' (an individual). In this metaphor, "island" becomes a metaphier carried over to re-define the human metaphand in the new individualist bourgeois way, a view that the older Donne rejects.

But there are other levels to this metaphor, whether its central conceptual statement is referred to approvingly or disapprovingly. Behind the signified concept/metaphier "island", we can find two HOMONYMS (Gk. *homos*=same; signs that sound the same but denote different things) which work as reinforcing metaphiers to the central concept:

a)   "Island" can be heard as "I land", here being the image of a new social order of individuals, which the older Donne as upholder of corporate, not isolated, individualism, rejects;

b)   "Island" also can be heard as "eye land", another aspect of the new individualism, in which we see the assumption of the individual viewer in perspectival Renaissance art.

Metaphor and Metonymy

Literary criticism commonly treats metaphor and metonymy as two literary figures which can be found in most literary texts. However, this approach fails to confront the profound implications of metaphor and metonymy as MODES OF THOUGHT which transcend the literary text. These modes of thought inform our structures of perception, the mental structures through which we proceed to construct all our textual worlds, including that of literature.

A slightly more sophisticated view associates metonymy with Science and Truth, and metaphor with Literature and the world of Fictions. This approach treats a scientific law as a micronym, a textual part which, it believes, precisely re-presents in scientific discourse the whole objective system or macronym of which it is said to be an essential part. From within this belief system or discourse, metaphor as a system of thought, a way of seeing, looks very imprecise because it defines one object or process (the metaphand) in terms of another object or process (the metaphier) which is not from the same semantic domain. This leaves room for the suspicion that subjective manipulations may be going on in the mediating process between the metaphier chosen and the metaphand to be defined. However, we cannot help but note the possibility that, wilfully or otherwise, metonymy can be subject to the same kinds of problems.

Metonymy, in fact, is not necessarily more precise than metaphor, assuming for the moment that absolute precision is either desirable or possible in descriptions. Moreover, metaphor can turn into metonymy and metonymy into metaphor with a change of presuppositions over time. Medieval and early Renaissance society saw the human body metonymously as a micronym of the macronymic nature, a living thing with precise microcosmic correspondences between it and macrocosmic nature. The new science of the sevententh century considered this former metonymic correspondence to be an erroneous metaphor. In its stead, the seventeenth century developed a mechanistic view of nature as machine. The clockwork became the metonym for the macrocosmic machine. Indeed, the human body came to be seen as a machine in the early pages of Hobbes' *Leviathan*, though the notion appears there as tentative metaphor. In doing so, Hobbes has rapidly reintroduced (within a different set of parameters) the notion of the anthropos as a microcosm of the cosmos. For B. F. Skinner, in our time, Hobbes' metaphor has become metonym. Meanwhile, cosmology, under the influence of Newton, took the machine metaphor and turned it into quantified mathematical formulae, metonyms said to be good for all time. It begins to look as if this Newtonian system is a metonym in terms of our local planetary system, but a metaphor when viewed from the perspective of the still not understood larger (and very smaller sub-atomic) cosmic systems.

The traditional tidy separation of metonymy into Science and metaphor into Literature, dating from the seventeenth century, is now breaking down. We begin to discern in the post-modern age that a metonym is as likely to be problematic as a metaphor. Indeed, we begin to perceive that metonymy can give the illusion of having achieved absolute Truth, thus turning it into a presupposition of thought which does not need questioning. This explains why post-modern science has no difficulty with the notion of metaphor. Post-modern science rejects the notion of an objective observer and sees rather any participant in nature in a process of change, a situation which requires a constant readjustment of theory, which is to say a constant questioning of the presuppositions of thought. Live metaphor retains an interactive field between the metaphier in the world of discourse and the metaphand which is the object or process to be explained, and it thus foregrounds its tentative condition. Of course, nothing is safe against the threat of habituation to received ideas, and it is habituation rather than metaphor or metonymy that is the problem in perception.

Some Other Figures

Figures of Comparison

Allegory

> *Allegory*: L. *allegoria*=speaking otherwise than one seems to speak; "description of a subject under the guise of some other subject of aptly suggestive resemblance." [*O.E.D.*]

This is a process of double signification where one signified has one concrete meaning, and the other one has some spiritual or other import. A fourteenth-century secular (L. *saeculum*=this world, not sacred or other worldly) lyric begins:

> Maiden in the mor lay
> [a maiden lived on the moor]
> in the mor lay
> [lived on the moor]
> Sevenighte fulle
> [a full week]
> Maiden in the mor lay
> [a maiden lived on the moor]
> Sevenighte fulle and a day
> [a full week and a day]

This work can also be treated as a sacred (L. *sacrare*=not secular or profane, relating to religion) poem dealing allegorically with Mary, the virgin mother of Jesus. In a very different vein, ''Lady Pecunia'' in Medieval and Renaissance Literature works as an allegorical figure through which abstract money is given life so as to reveal its corrupting qualities.

Symbols

''Symbol'' comes from the Latin (*symbolum*) and Greek (*symbolon*, from *symballo*=to infer, conclude; sym for *syn*=with; *ballo*=to throw or put; thus, to put with). It has a number of meanings:

a)   a sign: musical sign, dollar sign, arrow or road sign, etc.;

b)   a verbal sign: signifier which signifies a concept of a thing;

c)   Symbolism came out of French literature in the 1880s and had a great impact on English Literature earlier in this century. The symbolist poets recognized, in a very tentative way, the ''constructed'' character of ''reality'' in the realist text. They set out, therefore, to construct an imagined transcendental, ideal and superior world to create a dualist ''this world'' and superior ''other world''. The symbolist poet mediated between these two supposed worlds, using re-signified concrete things and processes as symbols through which to point to the ''other'', newly-constituted transcendental world. The poet intuited that transcendental world and used his symbols to communicate his intuitions. Invariably the symbols are subjective and difficult to interpret because there is no ''common'' or ''shared'' body of symbols and signs for this ''other'' world (indeed, no other world for that matter), except in the individual imaginations which the symbols mediate.

Allusion

ALLUSION: L. *alludo*; *ad*=to; *ludo*=to play; to play upon, to allude.

a)   INDIRECT ALLUSION means that the writer believes his audience is so familiar with the intertextual reference that he does not have to be explicit.

b)   DIRECT ALLUSION refers directly to the intertextual source so that there is no mistaking the reference.

An advantage of allusion is that it can tap the power of the source, which makes it an economical means of communication. A problem with allusion is that in fragmented, pluralist, modern society the writer cannot know what large areas of his audience know, or do not know, and whether they will recognize *any* allusions, explicit or not.

Pun

This term was originally known to the Greeks as *paronomasia*. Simply stated, a pun is a play on signs in which the signifiers are the same or similar, but the signifieds are (often amusingly) different, e.g. "hiss and make up" for "kiss and make up".

More seriously, puns serve the oral and written function of disrupting linear discourse and calling into question the either/or linear logic that lies behind linear discourse. Whereas flat logic insists that A cannot be A and not A at the same time, puns strike several semantic levels simultaneously to bring together what either/or logic would consider as A and not A. Since A is not a unified entity as either/or logic likes to think, but rather a series of levels, the pun can be more precise than this logic, since it can strike accurately a number of these levels. The pun, then, can either simply disrupt or destroy the pretensions to authority of solemn linear discourse, or it can make a positive contribution by introducing precise levels on which apparently disparate objects or processes meet. Either/or logic has difficulty with a changing world because of its static assumptions about the identity of objects or processes. Not fettered in this way, puns can deal with change (even anticipate it) as it occurs. Of course, a whole text can be based on a pun.

Homonymy

Let us be with her wholly at all hours...

The signs "wholly" and "holy" in this line from Lampman's "On the Companionship with Nature" are homonymous. They share the same phonemes but not the same graphemes. Lampman's example becomes somewhat more complex when we note that we are involved in a peculiar translation of "wholly" here from written to spoken discourse. The graphic image "wholly" carries over the sense of wholeness it signifies while, by immediate phonetic association, it merges with "holy". Since the truly "holy" itself derives originally from the pre-Christian Old English "hal", meaning whole, Lampman merges "wholly" and "holy" to take us back before Christianity to mend the artificial division of man and Nature, body and soul, etc.

Multiple Signification

This refers to a single signifier or signifying unit which has several signifieds or concepts.

Ambiguity

The term AMBIGUITY (L. *ambiguus*, *ambigo*=to go about) commonly has negative associations, suggesting "of doubtful meaning, unclear, equivocal". In fact, multiple signification can be negative or positive. At its inception it can be CONSCIOUS or UNCONSCIOUS; and it can also be CONTROLLED (whether conscious or not) or UNCONTROLLED (whether conscious or not, i.e. ambiguous in the negative sense). Ambiguity may also be, in varying degrees, PRECISE or IMPRECISE.

Lampman employs multiple signification in his "To a Millionaire":

> The world in gloom and splendour passes by,
> And thou in the midst of it with brows that gleam,
> A creature of that old distorted dream
> That makes the sound of life an evil cry.

The signifier "world" here signifies all of:

a) world, earth, globe, the total geographical physical environment;

b) the universe;

c) the earth and its inhabitants;

d) the public, a particular society.

An unfixed but precisely multi-focused signifier "world" focusses on all these level simultaneously, to be narrowed down to (d) temporarily by "passes by". Obviously, the globe and the universe do not pass by in this sense, and so "world" must signify "public". The root sense of the sign "man" becomes appropriate here because the Anglo-Saxon *wearhold* ("world") came from *wer*, meaning "man", and *yldo*, meaning "an age", to constitute the "age of man". Here, then, an age of man passes by. In the second line, "and there in the midst of it", the neuter pronoun "it" carries on the multiple signification, since "it" could signify any of the four possibilities of "world".

We find another example of double signification in the relative pronoun "That" at the beginning of the fourth line: "That makes the sound of life an evil cry." The question becomes, what does "That" signify? Is it "A creature'' (from the third line) ''That makes'', or is it ''that old distorted dream'' (from the third line) ''That makes''? And the answer must be both of them, to include both the creature and the distorted dream, the ideology which shaped him.

Malapropism and Freudian Slips

epitaph

hear about Kraf

yup

got laid   once

too often

he was a genital man   too bad

really

The two voices (1/''hear about Kraf''; 2/''yup'') in this poem by Dennis Cooley make this piece dramatic. The juncture allows an emblematic shape (as in some poems of early seventeenth-century England) to create the triangular outline of a grave stone. An example of Menippean discourse (see p. 208), which has no respect for anything, sacred or profane, these words become not only what is said in conversation between two unidentified voices, but also the unlikely profane epitaph on the sacred grave stone in a church yard. This Menippean attitude takes advantage of the punning double signification ''genital'' and ''gentle''. We have here the deliberate use of malapropism or Freudian slip.

Malapropism comes from the French *mal a propos*, meaning ''inappropriate'', but more immediately from the character Mrs. Malaprop in Sheridan's eighteenth-century play, *The Rivals*, who constantly uses the wrong words. Yet again, and we cannot be sure what Cooley ''intended'', it could also be a double signification in the sense that this misuse of language is supposed to conjure up Mrs. Malaprop and Freud, as an example of a ''Freudian slip''. Freud took the view that there is a manifest content to our lives and a latent one, in which repressed thoughts and feeling exist. Occasionally, we will inadvertently let slip what really preoccupies us. Here we see ''gentle'' refer to the language of polite society and public discourse (what we conventionally, and untruthfully, say about someone), but ''genital'' refers to what we actually may be thinking or feeling about that person.

The poem also plays with double signification when it introduces gallows humour in the phrase "got laid" and "once too often", referring simultaneously to sexual intercourse and being put into his grave. Again, juncture, pitch and stress operate ambiguously, carefully confusing things to produce another example of multiple signification on top of all this:

got laid once // too often
(only once, and it was too often—sex)

got laid once too often
(a lot of times, one too many)

got laid / once / too often
(only one time, poor devil, and it was too much for him)

Litotes

LITOTES is a form of understatement which implies its opposite. Here, "He's no moron" means "He's bright".

Oxymoron

OXYMORON (Gk. *oxy*=sharp; *moros*=dull) is a union of contraries as in the Renaissance "fair-foul" woman.

Understatement

UNDERSTATEMENT is of two basic kinds:

a)   that which says much less than the objective situation requires: "Yes, my five-minute mile wasn't bad for a rank amateur";

b)   that which says much less when the event is truly significant: "My Nobel Prize? Just had to burn a bit of midnight oil, that's all."

Dictionaries, Denotation
and Atomic Physics

Classical Greek materialism re-entered the European intellectual mainstream in 1649 through the French philosopher Gassendus, whose "Life Of Epicurus" was also a defence of atomic theory. That year also saw the future founders of The Royal Society of London (the scientific institute) meeting in Oxford. While the older physics treated material reality as composed of varying combinations of the four elements (earth, water, air, and fire), the more elegant atomic theory treated the atom as the fundamental unit of matter. Indeed, "atom" means "indivisible" in Greek. This concept of the indivisible atom dominated our culture into the twentieth century which would conceptually, and actually, split the atom.

In the minds of the founders of The Royal Society, the "new" atomic theory from physics joined the underdetermined discourse of science. "Word" as a mathematically precise sign for a thing (denotation) became the equivalent of the unsplittable and unchanging atom.

This whole development soon produced the need for "authentic" definitions and dictionaries, which explains why the eighteenth century became the first great age of dictionaries. Ninety years after the founding of The Royal Society, the novelist Henry Fielding lamented that "All the major words are not to be found in dictionaries." Three years after Fielding, Dr. Johnson wrote in his 1755 dictionary: "I have attempted...a dictionary of the English language which, while it was employed in the calculation of every species of literature, has itself been hitherto neglected." The great ten-volume Oxford appeared in parts between 1884 and 1928.

Correct Spelling

With dictionaries came orthography (Gk. *orthos*=right; *graphein*=to write), the idea of "correct spelling". The ideology of "correct spelling" limits possibilities for using the material signifier system, and thus puts constraints on overdetermined discourse. Orthography favours underdetermined discourse, and helps to reify language in the form of "Standard English": that which is fixed we become habituated to, and do not see. Shakespeare wrote his own name in a variety of ways, revealing that he did not care about fixed orthography, though he knew of the concept.

The Present Spell

Advertisers and some poets in our age have split the orthographic atom, just as physicists have split the atom itself. Students today live more in a Shakespearean world of sound, irregular spelling and overdetermined discourse (the new media), and less in a world of sight, the book, correct spelling, and underdetermined discourse. They therefore—from the point of view of underdetermined discourse and orthodoxy—cannot spell, but that orthodoxy itself is relatively new. In fact, "spell" did not take on its orthographic meaning until 1702.

The Spell of Ideology

People have dislocated or disrupted spelling practices in the recent past (correct spelling) for a variety of reasons:

a)   because they do not know any better, which is to say because they have not been inscribed with the idea of correct spelling;

b)   because they have been exposed more to the irregular spelling practices of advertisers than to conventional texts and correct spelling;

c)   because advertisers deliberately misspell in order to defamiliarize people, making it easier to take the reader into a familiar-unfamiliar world of glitter and promise;

d)   because some modern poets wish to break up signs as they break up line units. They do this in order to create new expressive capabilities, ones capable of presenting simultaneously a new multiplicity of meanings in the textual world.

What is Literature?

The question "What is Literature?" (L. *litteratura* from *littera*, a letter) assumes the existence of the object which it wishes to interrogate. It thus prepares the way for a preconceived answer of the kind: "Literature is X."

A Metaphysical Concept

As employed in the question above, the sign "Literature" is a metaphysical concept (Gk. *meta*=beyond; *physis*=material; beyond the material; L. *conceptus*, a collecting, a gathering, a thought, a generalized idea of a class of objects). It is a very high-level abstraction which gets reified (L. *res*=thing) and comes to be taken as a thing in itself.

Constituting the Object

Writers of all kinds work with certain kinds of discourses to produce political, sociological, religious, and all the other texts that make up all the books and newspapers and journals in a society. They write according to, or in revolt against, the culturally constructed conventions of their discourse. Critical acts of all kinds create categories of classification which separate Literature from literature. This is the first way in which literature gets constituted, made, into Literature, through the critical act of naming and classifying.

The second phase in the constitution of Literature as Literature occurs when the critical act divides Literary works into Great Literature, i.e. Authentic Literature, as it likes to think, and the rest of Literature, i.e. the vast mass of "non-authentic" Literature. This mass includes work which, by any standards, would be considered "bad work", but it also includes various kinds of hyphenated Literature such as Children's-Literature, Pop-Literature and so on.

The Canon

The sign "canon" descends to us from the Latin *canon* which meant "a measuring line", and went on to become, in religious terminology, the name for the list of allowed or approved scriptures. Canon is the name given to the constituted list of "Great" works of Literature, the result of acts of exclusion, and it still retains a sense of sacred scripts. The notion of canon and exclusion has come under heavy attack in the twentieth century.

The Literary Object

The Literary artifact is an object with an objective material existence independent of the subject-reader. In this sense it is like the physical universe.

Constituting the Literary Object

As we have seen, a Literary object becomes a Literary object only through an act of critical constitution that makes it such.

Constituting the "I"

As we constitute the Literary object through the act of reading and critical decision, so does it constitute us so far as we allow it to, either by questioning our vision of the world and changing it, or by affirming values we already have. The writer goes through a similar process as he gives shape to his vision in the creation of a text.

Massaging & Messaging, Readerly & Writerly Texts

A massaging or readerly text will affirm values we already have and thus leave us undisturbed, while a writerly and messaging text will in some way disrupt our settled expectations.

Liking a Literary Object

Not liking a Literary object may mean that in some way it is a "bad" Literary object, or that the reader is sitting in his/her garden on a sunny Sunday afternoon prepared only to read massaging readerly texts (e.g. popular romances), but confronts a disruptive writerly messaging text instead. Other readers in their armchairs expecting experimental messaging and writerly texts will be equally upset to find only massaging and readerly texts available.

What the Literary Text Is Not

A Literary object is not an example of religious, political, or psychological discourse, but a Literary one, a structure of structures and sub-structures of material, overdetermined language. Yet a Literary Text will be political in a deeper sense of the term, in that it has to do with values generated in life in the polis (Gk. *polis*=city state).

Determinacy and Indeterminacy of Meaning

There are three basic views with respect to this subject:

a)   Every Literary text is determined, has a predetermined meaning which the reader or critic seeks to discover;

b)   Every Literary text is indeterminate, having no predetermined meaning, so the reader or critic can impose or discover whatever meaning he/she wishes;

c)   Over a period of historical time and/or place, any specific Literary text may lend itself to a variety of readings, but the text itself has boundaries set by its structures and codes, and these latter limit the range of possible meanings.

We can make several brief observations about these positions:

a)   We must not fall into the trap of the fallacy of the ideal reader. There is no ideal reader—only individuals with different ranges of reading competence and general experience. Here is an oversimplified example: for the uninitiated (someone who does not know the structures and codes of Literature beyond the literal level of plot and character), Joseph Conrad's *Heart of Darkness* is a literal travel/adventure story. For the initiated, it becomes a journey into the problematic of Euro-American civilization itself (hence its later double in the film *Apocalypse Now!*). On this level, the text then becomes a battleground of contending religious, existentialist, Marxist, etc. interpretations. Here, the larger socio-economic conflicts of our time are worked out in the realms of culture, each position seeking to gain control over and deny validity to the others.

b)   If the reader is a SOLIPSIST (L. *solus ipse*=himself alone; one who believes the world exists only in his own imagination, and his imagination alone), then obviously this reader would assume that all persons would have different understandings of a text. However, since solipsists cannot by definition communicate their individual attempts at constructing meaning to any other persons, we may leave them to their solitary dreams.

c)   A Literary text exists "out there", as does nature for the Newtonian/ Cartesian scientist. In both cases, the understanding of the object can only be shaped through the presuppositions of thought that we take with us when we start our studies. These presuppositions set a limit on what we can see, although they can, with difficulty, be changed.

d)   When we study the Literary object, we involve ourselves in the translation of one form of discourse into another: the translation of the discourse of Literature into the discourse of Criticism. The Literary object can never be brought over in its entirety through translation, so inevitably with every translation something is left behind, something which later changes in perception will cause to be seen. This means neither that our present reading is inadequate, nor that we are heading for a telos or goal which will be *the* final and single understanding. The same situation pertains in science.

e)   Constraints are placed on the number of possible meanings of a text by the structures and codes of that text. Ignorance, wilful or otherwise, leaves room for either very few or a great number of meanings, but as texts are deconstructed and decoded to reveal hitherto unseen parts of their skeletal frames, a limit is placed on the wild variety of these supposed meanings, without bringing down closure.

f)   To insist on a single meaning for a text, which is tantamount to insisting on a single correct translation of the text, one good for all time, is to impose closure on that text, and thus to declare it dead. To insist that any number of meanings are possible declares the text irrelevant, since there would be nothing of particular human interest in the text. To see criticism as a continual and never-ending process of studying an object which, like nature itself, continues to mutate, means that there must be an ongoing decoding and resignifying of texts. This occurs as new Literary texts are mediated through critical practice, throwing new light on both old Literary texts and old critical practices. The whole enterprise throws light on what it is to be involved in human discourse at a particular point in time and space.

Ongoing Process

In life and in Literary texts, the human psyche and socio-economic structures, indeed literary texts themselves, may be described as systems in ongoing process. Three such systems of ongoing process from Anthony Wilden's *System and Structure* concern us here: homeostasis, homeorhesis, and morphogenesis. To these we can add another which might be called homeokenosis.

The domestic heating system controlled by a thermostat serves as a classical example of homeostasis (Gk. *homos*=the same; *statikos*=to stand, in balance). A disturbance upsets equilibrium to create disequilibrium in the thermostat—a result of an environmental change. The thermostat sends a negative feedback to the furnace instructing it to produce more heat. Heat circulates throughout the environment to raise the temperature, remove the disequilibrium, and restore equilibrium in this closed system. Programmed as a closed system, the thermostat cannot send a positive feedback instructing the furnace to change its structure, its way of responding owing to some extraordinary shift in the environment. We may illustrate the homeostatic closed system in the following way:

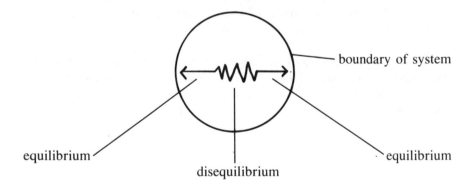

Meg and Petey in Pinter's *The Birthday Party* are two homeostatic minds who represent a homeostatic society. In Meg and Petey, Pinter creates two characters who endure the disturbance caused by the arrival of Goldberg and McCann and their forcible removal of Stanley. At the end of the play, however, they move from disequilibrium back to the equilibrium with which they started, revealing no sign of having learned anything, or of having changed their structures of perception in any way. While these characters are homeostatic, the play itself is morphogenetic, as we shall see below.

In homeorhesis, we find development of structure occurring within fixed limits or boundaries. In contrast to the closed homeostatic system, this form of ongoing process can send positive feedback to change its own structure, but only within the limits set by the boundaries of the system. In terms of psychic structures, this form of learning process can give the illusion of complete freedom, until the mind hits the outer boundaries and becomes forced to face as unsupported presuppositions what had seemed to be absolute truths or givens. We can illustrate homeorhesis as follows:

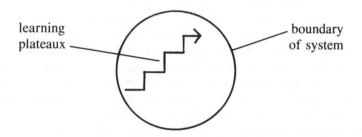

learning plateaux

boundary of system

In Leacock's "The Conjurer's Revenge", the braggart Quick Man or alazon is a homeostatic character with an extremely rigid psychic structure that resists change. Thus, when the social environment changes as the Conjurer gets his revenge by turning to dirty tricks (under the guise of a conjuring trick) by actually smashing the Quick Man's watch, the Quick Man cannot adjust, learn, see what is happening. The conjurer defeats the Quick Man precisely because he can learn and adjust to a changed and hostile environment. When he discovers that the Quick Man will never stop disrupting his performance, the Conjurer ceases being a conjurer on stage and becomes a vengeful human being, a homeorhetic transformation which the homeostatic Quick Man cannot discern.

With morphogenesis (Gk. *morphos* = shape) a homeorhetic system hits its own outer boundaries and makes a metaphorical and morphogenetic leap out of the old structure to create a new one. We may illustrate this in the following way:

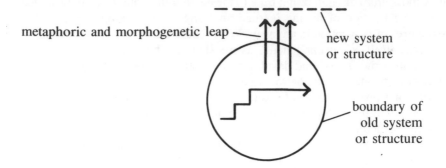

We might say that Einstein made such a leap out of the old Newtonian cosmological structure, with its assumption of time and space as containers, into the creation of a new one which sees reality as a four-dimensional space-time continuum. Without Goldberg and McCann in the middle of Pinter's *The Birthday Party*, but with more mundane realist replacements for them, the play would be a homeostatic kitchen-sink realist text which moved from equilibrium to disequilibrium back to equilibrium with nothing essentially changed. The presence of the surrealist or fantasy text, represented by the disruptive Goldberg and McCann, however, makes the play in fact an open-ended or dialogical text without monological closure and without a single level of meaning. The form of what would have been a realist text, therefore, undergoes a change of shape to make the play itself an example of morphogenetic ongoing process. In relation to the homeostatic Meg and Petey, and the homeorhetic Conjurer in the Leacock story, Goldberg and McCann are morphogenetic characters, fragmented, polymorphous pysches as opposed to unified egos.

Arnason's "Sylvie" (pp. 198-221) is an excellent example of homeokenosis (Gk. *kenosis*=self-emptying). In this homeokenotic text both the psyche of the speaker and the image of his civilization that emerges look like recognizably solid structures on the outside, but on the inside both the mind and the civilization have been drained of authentic human content to leave them empty shells.

Morley Callaghan's *Such is My Beloved* offers a range of characters in a conflict of ongoing processes. The young liberal idealist priest, Father Dowling, models himself after Christ among the poor. He seeks to help two (homeostatic) poverty-stricken girls who have been forced into prostitution out of financial need. Blind to the existence of boundaries to his Church system, he sets out in homeorhetic fashion to do good on the assumption that he is free.

The Bishop and Mr. Robison, a rich lawyer and capitalist, represent the homeostatic establishment and its desire to maintain respectability and the economic status quo. They are the homeostatic outer boundaries of Dowling's homeorhetic system that he will run into and be defeated by. While Dowling feels free to act, he is in fact being tolerated temporarily as a disturbance by the Bishop and the lawyer within the framework of their homeostatic world system. We may see Dowling from the point of view of the establishment as follows:

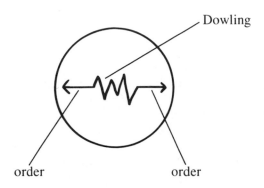

When the establishment brings down closure on him, Dowling finds himself in a double-bind situation: if he moves forward into a morphogenetic new system, he will defy the Bishop and hence have to leave his beloved Church. If he stays in the Church and obeys the Bishop he must give up the model of Christ among the poor. The problem drives him mad. Meanwhile, his friend Charlie serves as a model of a morphogenetic leap forward into a new world system, that of communism. It seems clear, however, that this leap by Charlie is mainly on the level of mind, for the Bishop and the rich lawyer will ensure that orthodoxy prevails.

Genre

The sign GENRE (Gk. *genos*) has the same origins as the scientific term "genus", and serves the same classificatory purpose. It came into English from the French immediately after the Napoleonic Wars. There are three basic positions possible with respect to genre theory, only one of which will pass the tests of free and democratic practice:

a)   the metaphysical approach;

b)   the vulgar materialist approach;

c) the approach of praxis and fuzzy or open-ended logic.

The Metaphysical Approach

The metaphysical approach appears to deal with both the concreteness and the historical fact of works of literature. The term itself comes from the Greek (*meta*=beyond; *physis*=physics) and it originally meant "the book by Aristotle which follows the book on Physics in his Works". Subsequently, it has come to mean high level abstractions, signified concepts on the level of thought and language, with no discernible significatum or reference object in the empirical world. Rather, the metaphysical definition ruthlessly constitutes its objects by forcing them into preconceived static molds.

The metaphysical approach therefore creates an abstract definition, based on empirical observations of SOME IDENTITIES between a number of Literary works, and correctly allows for the discovered similarities. It proceeds to go wrong when it REPRESSES DIFFERENCES between those Literary works and thus falsifies the evidence. Moreover, this definition through identities is then reified (a concept confused with a thing). Like a South American dictator, the metaphysical approach to genre soon begins to impose a rigid order on Literature, insisting that "X" is literature while "Y" is not, in general serving to prevent recognition of the new in Literature.

Each CANONICAL TEXT in the metaphysical approach thus becomes a double text, one of PRESENCE on the level of identities, and one of ABSENCE, a shadow text, on the level of REPRESSED differences.

The Vulgar Materialist Approach

The vulgar materialist approach cannot really be considered an approach at all, for it:

a) looks at the way the metaphysical approach represses differences between texts to force identities;

b) looks at the way the dictatorial metaphysical approach refuses to recognize new works that do not fit into the (false) categories;

c) looks at the huge Literary inheritance from the past, and the body of twentieth-century work which deliberately mixes genre in an act of Literary miscegenation (poets seek in this way to avoid being falsely categorized or categorized at all);

d) throws up its hands. It concludes that nothing can be done since it considers

Literary works finally to be unclassifiable. If the metaphysical view is that of the absolutist dictator, the vulgar materialist view emerges as that of popular anarchy.

The Approach of Praxis and Fuzzy or Open-Ended Logic

The Greek term PRAXIS refers to a self-regulating system (here Literary production) in which theory (past practice codified) guides practice, while present practice adds to and modifies theory. This approach avoids both the theocratic (Gk. *theos*=God) obsession with single and fixed definitions of the metaphysical approach, and the anarchy of the vulgar materialist one.

From the angle of praxis we codify works generically through fuzzy or open-ended logic and the theory of equivalences. We note that a work is a hierarchy of levels (this hierarchy is metaphor) and that different works can be the same—belong to the same class—without being absolutely identical. They can be identical on some levels and different on others. Moreover, in this system there can be no privileged positions, a fact which relieves the writer in the present of the psychological burden of being constantly subordinated to writers of the past. The system has an easy and democratic plenitude about it. This allows it to accept new and different works because of the dialectical way in which new works, on the level of practice, will regulate theory by changing it.

We start analysis with a text from a genre, when the genre first appears "fully developed" in history. Without privileging that text in the sense of assuming its total characteristics to be definitive, we note the characteristics on all levels of the text that make it what it is. Then we take works from across history which are similar, and note the similarities and differences. We do this with a view to determining the cultural reasons (e.g. major shifts in the presuppositions of thought in an age) for significant changes in form. With the sonnet, for example, we would find a strong emphasis on control of the emotions over the centuries down to the present, with clear indications of a freeing up or disintegration of the classic form as rhyme disappears (in advanced usage), and syntax becomes fragmented (e.g. Roethke). By scanning the various evolutions of the form in this fashion, we could, so to speak, X-ray our culture in motion.

Metre, Rhythm and the Unified "I"

Characters appear not only in the discourse of prose fiction, but in the discourse of poetry as well: in long narrative poetry, in poetic drama, and in lyric poetry. For the persona in lyric poetry is a character too, one constructed out of the deepest presuppositions with respect to character and kinds of discourse in a particular age. We shall be concerned here with the textual construction of character as both the lyric persona and the narrator in poetry over the past thousand or so years. This process of the investigation of character construction will take us into, by conventional standards, the strangest places, starting with the ideological foundations of poetic rhythms.

A Partial Preview

Following Antony Easthope and his *Poetry as Discourse* (and others whose work is cited there), we see iambic pentameter as a new ideological metrical form, defeating the old Anglo-Saxon rhythms, at the beginning of the sixteenth century. We then witness, at the beginning of the twentieth century, the attempt by Ezra Pound and others to give the iamb "the heave". This poetic act of trying to break the control of the "iamb" forms part of an attack on the unified ego of the "I am" variety. This act, on the part of modernism, began the conflict over poetic form and character which still rages, with uneasy truces being maintained under the flag of a pluralistic culture.

Handbooks of Poetics

Handbooks of poetics frequently create unnecessary difficulties in at least three areas when they deal with poetic rhythms: first, they commonly fail to distinguish between rhythm and metre; second, they do not discern that some Literary historical periods are concerned with rhythm without—consciously or unconsciously—being aware of metre (in the sense to be defined), while others are concerned—either consciously or unconsciously—with both metre and rhythm; third, handbooks speak of four kinds of rhythm, without drawing out the implications of their awareness that two are totally or almost totally irrelevant with respect to English poetics. These problems are the source of great confusion.

Rhythm and Metre

METRE derives from the Greek *metron*, "a measure", while RHYTHM comes from the Greek *rhythmos*, which means "measured motion", and descends from the Greek verb *rhein*, which means to flow. For our purposes "metre" emerges as the ideal (meaning not "best", but a "mental concept") and fixed measuring standard, while rhythm emerges as "the measured flow" which metre, in the mind, measures. Metre refers to Plato's transcendental (beyond experience) realm of the IDEA, out of its time and space. Rhythm refers to the imperfect (relative to the impossible ideal) form that metre assumes when it adopts a material linguistic and discourse shape in a world of change.

English: Two Kinds of Rhythm

There are essentially two kinds of rhythm in English, what we shall— without reference to other languages or practices—here call:

a)   quantitative: this involves both metre and rhythm and revolves around iambic pentameter;

b)   qualitative: this form involves only rhythm.

Classification

When we turn to Literary History we immediately confront the problem of classification. The traditional way of classifying English Literature tends to obscure important continuities amid the changes of history, as well as to suppress the full significance of some of those changes. No system of classification, of course, has proved to be adequate for all purposes, and perhaps no single system ever can be adequate. After all, systems of classification require choices about inclusion and exclusion. Such (finally arbitrary) choices inevitably introduce the question of value, and value, being subjective, throws so-called objectivity out the door. To avoid some problems, we shall follow here the practice of post-modern science and not be concerned about the truth value of our schema in the sense of absolutes. We shall simply be concerned with the question of what kind of useful results our classifications might produce. Accordingly, for heuristic purposes, we divide the last thousand or more years into three parts:

> I   -1529: qualitative (excepting the precocious Chaucer)
> II 1529-1910: quantitative
> III   1910-: qualitative & quantitative

The Early Qualitative Phase To 1529

We shall proceed here to a simple view of the early qualitative phase, noting key changes and continuities.

Anglo-Saxon

The following lines come from Caedmon's "Hymn":

> Nu sculon herigan   heofonerices weard
> metodes meahte   and his modge thanc
> weorc wuldorfaeder   swa he wundra gewas

These lines remain all but completely unrecognizable to untrained modern minds, because the Anglo-Saxon does not have a linear subject-verb-object syntax. We note, however, the alliterative rhythm of the first line, which stresses only the two syllables beginning with "h", two stresses out of twelve syllables:

$$\overset{/}{\text{Nu // scul / on // her / i / gan //////}} \overset{/}{\text{he / o / fon / e / ric / es // we / ard}}$$

The three initial "m" syllables get stressed out of eleven in line two, and the three "w" syllables out of twelve in line three.

Middle English

Structural changes in the language over a few hundred years produced a linear syntax and discourse which makes later work accessible to the untrained modern mind. This we discover with ''Sir Gawain and the Green Knight'' from somewhere in the middle of the 1300s:

   /   /   /   /
Sithen the sege ond the assaut was cesed at Troye
(After the seige and the assault was ceased at Troy)

The Gawain line looks backwards and forwards, forwards to what will become the linear clarity (for us) of the Shakespeare sonnets, and backwards to the alliterative old Anglo-Saxon. (The reference to looking forwards here should not be taken to imply the necessity of the changes that led to Shakespeare. What happened could have been arrested at any point in history). This first line from the Gawain poem has fourteen syllables (the last ''e'' is a syllable), but only four stresses, which occur on the ''s'' syllables.

The last important user of this ACCENTUAL rhythm until recent times, though not the alliterative variety, was John Skelton (1460?-1529):

    /
Pla ce bo

   /   /   /
Who is there, who?

  / / /   /
Fa, re, my, my,

    /   /   /
Wherefore and why, why?

      /   /   /
For the soul of Phillip Sparrow,

        /   /   /
That was late slain at Carrow

    /   /   /
Among the nunnes blacke.

        /   /   /
For that sweet soule's sake

        /   /   /
And for all sparrows' souls

   /   /
Set in our bead rolls

This has yet greater clarity, with a clear sense of linearity for the modern mind, and a rhythmic order, despite the fact that the number of syllables and the number of rhythmic stresses in the line cannot be predicted.

Qualitative Time and Rhythm

We find in the QUALITATIVE ACCENTUAL RHYTHMS of the Anglo-Saxon and Middle English poems the poetic-linguistic equivalent of QUALITATIVE TIME. This qualitative time was the time of organic agricultural societies which had not yet been subjected to the quantification of mechanical clock time. In agricultural societies close to nature, time flows in a manner not unlike the experience we have when we "lose ourselves" (i.e. escape the regimentation of clock time) at parties and so on. But most of us live in urban environments in which street lighting turns night into day, while central heating and air-conditioning standardize our existence by making all days climatically the same. Meanwhile clocks measure out our work days, appointments, time to see a film, and precise calendars mark our births and deaths. The so-called (unfortunately pejorative) "Indian time" of North American native peoples is one version of qualitative time. In qualitative time no two days ever appear exactly alike, while seasons shift and change their lengths year after year. This qualitative poetic rhythm thus reproduced in its users and listeners the qualitative sense of time which all the members of all the estates and classes shared. In its very rhythmic structures it caused the reproduction of a communal value, that of qualitative time (a form of measure) in its audience.

Qualitative Time and Character

A specific sense of time works as one of the shaping presuppositions of an age. People take time to be natural, and fail to observe its cultural origins. We see this in the reference to "Indian time" above, itself a cultural construct arising out of the concrete experiences of the mainstream of Euro-American culture perceiving a difference in native cultures' experience of time. "Indian time", by contrast, defines "White man's time", because if the proverbial Indian has trouble "being on time", then that says something about Euro-American concepts of time. As Lewis Mumford pointed out over fifty years ago in *Technics and Society*, clock time came out of those laboratories of industrialism and regimentation, the monasteries of the late Middle Ages. The Euro-American has therefore been interiorizing the sense of clock time for over 600 years, and that happened in the context of the historical constitution of the unified "I" within the framework of the metanarrative of progress. The North American Indian peoples have been subjected to clock time for a much briefer period.

Along with his different, qualitative, sense of time, the unincorporated native Indian has a different sense of self. The highly disproportionate number of native people cramming prairie jails in Canada testifies to, among other things, the absence in these people of a unified bourgeois "I". This means that these persons do not have a sense of the body as property. And certainly they do not have the acquisitive respect for private property which goes with the sense of self as property. Their sense of self and time moves much closer to those of Medieval Europeans, where the limits on the range of possible actions by any person were not as narrowly constrained as those which operate to contain the unified bourgeois "I".

Community, Sound, and Corporate Individualism

The alliterative poetry, designed for performance as sound in a closed community, differs from poetry designed for reading through sight by a reader. As Walter Ong shows so well in *Orality and Literacy*, the former is a collective medium of performance, the latter an individual enterprise. The collectivity, which was the listening audience, joined with the poet in qualitative poetic rhythm and time as flow, to help reproduce in the community the corporate individualism of collective feudal society. The deeper levels of this collective or corporate individualism can only emerge for us after we have looked at metre and rhythm in quantitative verse.

1529-1910

On the level of content, we can easily find abundant evidence of an awareness of the independent bourgeois self as property, as unified ego, and of the kind of property relationships discussed earlier in poems of this period. Here follows an example from Shakespeare ("Sonnet 87"):

Farewell—thou art too dear for my possessing,
And like enough thou knowest thine estimate;
The charter of thy worth gives thee releasing;
My bonds in thee are all determinate.
For how do I hold thee but by thy granting?
And for what riches where is my deserving?
The cause of this fair gift in me is wanting,
And so my patent back again is swerving.
Thy self thou gavest, thy own worth then not knowing;
. Or me, to whom thou gavest it, else mistaking:
So thy great gift, upon misprision growing,
Comes home again on better judgement making.
   Thus I had thee as a dream doth flatter:
   In sleep a king, but waking no such matter.

Social Reproduction of the "I"

Shakespeare fills the "Farewell" sonnet with monetary and property references. But it is not alone on the level of content, of signified conceptual meaning, that this speaker/character reveals himself. As with the conflicts over value in novels and other texts, this text works at a deeper level. At that level the text causes a reproduction of the reader as unified ego and isolated individual, while revealing the speaker/character as the same. If we take another sonnet ("Sonnet 64") much less obviously about property, we can probe the deeper depths:

> When I / have seen / by Time's / fell hand / defaced /
> The rich / proud cost / of out / worn bur / ied age /
> When some / time lof / ty towers / I see / down razed /
> And brass / eter / nal slave / to mort / al rage /
> When I / have seen / the hung / ry oc / ean gain /
> Advan / tage on / the king / dom of / the shore /
> And the / firm soil / won of / the wate / ry main /
> Increas / ing store / with loss / and loss / with store /
> When I / have seen / such in / ter change / of state /
> Or state / it self / confound / ed to / decay /
> Ruin / hath taught / me thus / to rum / inate /
> That time / will come / and take / my love / away /
>> This thought / is as / a death / which can / not choose /
>> But weep / to have / that which / it fears / to lose /

Having divided the sonnet into its metrical feet, we must bracket the level of the signifieds and forget, for the moment, about conceptual meaning. We are concerned now with the abstract level of the material signifiers in relation to each other: specifically the abstract units of the metrical feet. These we may represent as follows in abstract mathematical terms:

1	2	3	4	5
6	7	8	9	10
11	12	13	14	15
16	17	18	19	20
21	22	23	24	25
26	27	28	29	30
31	32	33	34	35
36	37	38	39	40
41	42	43	44	45
46	47	48	49	50
51	52	53	54	55
56	57	58	59	60
61	62	63	64	65
66	67	68	69	70

This poem has two dimensions, the quantitative and the qualitative. Quantitative metre is abstractly represented by the silences of the grid pattern, and qualitative rhythm by the numbers. Metre as the transcendental Idea of order gets imposed from without to control the tendency of imperfect language to flow in an unruly rhythmic manner (''unruly'' is so, of course, from the questionable point of view of those who desire rigid order, wherein someone or something ''rules'').

Perfection and Imperfection

If we were to attempt to portray the unportrayable (perfection cannot be portrayed in any way) metrical *ideal*, we would start as follows:

I	II	III	IV	V
⌣ /	⌣ /	⌣ /	⌣ /	⌣ /

This assumes that the three components of the iambic metre are perfectly identical on their various levels: each soft stress identical, each hard stress identical, and each silent space between stresses identical. The materiality of language, however, will not allow the realization of this ideal of perfection. Material signs in our language do not have equal and recognizable values, and we cannot force them into the ''ideal'' mould without making communication either ridiculous or impossible. We can, however, illustrate what happens in practice, by contrast with the above representation of perfection. Here we shall impose a one-to-four scale degree of stress on both the hard and soft stresses, a common procedure in the analysis of rhythm:

	I		II		III		IV		V	
1				•				•			
2	•					•					•
3		•	•					•		•	
4					•						
	∪	/	∪	/	∪	/	∪	/	∪	/

The imperfection of the stresses points to the unruliness of material language, while the grid pattern indicates that the main mechanism of control is the grid pattern itself, which is to say, the NETWORK or GRID OF SILENCES. The inner qualitative dimension accepts the uneven and rugged quality of signs in all their materiality, while the containing and structuring abstract grid from without quantifies and controls the flow of signs, and hence restrains ("rules" or "governs") the unruliness. Transcendental metrical control thus inhibits the immanental (within things) flow of rhythm. The qualitative Anglo-Saxon and Middle English (though Chaucer and his precocious iambics anticipate the control of the sixteenth century) has no concept of metre or outside control in this fashion.

Cartography and Control

Quantitative metre came from outside and preceded the act of poetic creation as a device for carefully and silently controlling rhythmic flow. At the same time, the cartographers (L. *charta*, Gk. *graphein*; mapmakers) associated with the so-called voyages of exploration imposed pre-existent Euclidean geometry on unruly nature. They quantified and made manageable the material world on a global scale (a process still being extended into cosmic space):

Perspective: The ''I'' and the Eye

In much the same way, the development of perspective in painting took pre-existent Euclidean geometry and imposed it on nature. This created a new ''realist'' way of seeing. The majority of people today—nearly all naive realists—still believe pictorial realism to be an actual representation of the ''real'', the thing of nature itself, rather than one form of discourse or way of seeing among others:

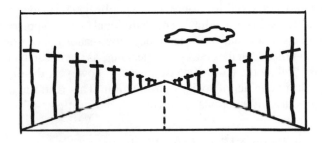

Mathematics of Control

The use of numbers along with the grid pattern in the Shakespeare sonnet above was no accident. We see the rise of mathematics in the sixteenth century at the hands of Heriot and others, a development which would allow Newton in the seventeenth century to mathematicize, and control, the hitherto somewhat unruly heavens.

The Politics of Control

Behind all these connections between methods of control lies the political.

We have surely to ask why the court of Henry VIII should single out the sonnet form as THE lyric form for special development over others. In Lyric, a form of discourse, an individual speaker looks at some aspect of life from a personal point of view, but only as far as the discourse will allow.

As an absolute monarch, Henry recalled well the hundred years of civil war which his father had finally put to rest when he successfully claimed absolute power, and thereby created the basis for continued absolute nation-state power embodied in the king. He remained aware also of potential challenges to that power from disgruntled and proud members of the ruling caste. These persons still considered a king as merely the first amongst equals in accordance with the conditions of the Magna Carta of 1215. And so Henry set out to civilize this proud and unruly mob. He gave them a new culture by encouraging the importation of Italian culture into his court. There the courtiers would learn dance, music, poetry, and learn also to restrain their impetuous wills while keeping their noses out of *his* politics.

Interestingly, the only one of the early Tudor court sonneteers to have trouble with imposing abstract metrical control on flowing rhythm frequently found himself in political trouble with Henry: Sir Thomas Wyatt.

Time and Reproducing the ''I''

Shakespeare did not write his sonnets for public performance to a group audience, but for solitary reading. The individual reader approaches these poems as objects at a distance. In tendency, the reader concentrates on the sequence of signifieds, on the conceptual meaning, as the linear syntax unfolds the signifieds. Below the level of consciousness, however, the metrical grid restrains rhythm in an act of social reproduction. This restraint on emotion helps to reproduce an emotionally restrained and unified ''I''.

The Transcendental ''I'' and the Intellect

What we see emerging in these sonnets of the sixteenth century is the intellect isolated from emotion. This intellect will become more or less fully separable from emotion over time, to allow the development of the plain prose underdetermined discourse of science (and ''non-fiction'').

Time, the ''I'' and Atomism

The continually different flow of the Middle English qualitative accentual rhythms followed the flow patterns of qualitative time in a state close to the variety of nature. Quantified metre breaks the poem into more or less identical atomic quantitative units, units which anticipate the atomism of Gassendi later in the mid-seventeenth century. These units follow the pattern of clock time, and constitute a geometrical grid pattern which controls language. Indeed, the alliteration and assonance and iambic rhythms in another Shakespeare sonnet ("Sonnet 12") actually announce this connection with clock time:

⏑ / ⏑ / ⏑ / ⏑ / ⏑ /
When I do count the clock that tells the time

The combination of iambic rhythms along with alliteration and assonance makes this line tick out the signified clock of which it speaks.

Unified Control

We see, then, that with the absolute political power which shaped people and a new political state came:

Geometry ——————— perspectival painting ——————— empirical world
Geometry———————————maps & globes———————————empirical world
Poemetry ——————————— poems ——————————— empirical world

In all these instances it was not a matter of DESCRIBING the empirical world, *but of constituting, literally making it new* through using geometry and poemetry as new ways of seeing. And by the existence of these new bourgeois forms, older ways of seeing were destroyed. The new forms of control mark the rise of bourgeois hegemony within the framework of the centralized monarchy. Reality was being completely resignified.

The Unified Individual

Abstract Euclidean geometry in the minds of its users was a way of seeing which the Renaissance painters imposed upon the textual discourse of painting, though for the longest time it has been, in naive realist fashion, considered to be a neutral way of grasping the "real" thing: nature. What it did, however, was to build into perspectival art works a privileged viewing position for the isolated individual. Feudal art presented no such privileged position because it was designed to reproduce corporate individualism. This new privileged single viewing position invited the isolated individual first to become aware of his own body as property, and then to step into the privileged viewing position of power so as to take possession of the visual space and the art object as property. This process is much like that of the European "discoverers" who, with their grid-dominated new maps, were taking possession of land and wealth on a number of continents.

The Shakespeare poem presupposes an isolated individual poet as perspectival art had presupposed an isolated individual painter. As the painter and cartographer applied an abstract geometry onto the space of nature to produce landscapes and maps respectively from a single point of view, so did the poet lay this grid of the repeatable metrical foot on the sonnet. Moreover, as the geometry pre-existed the "space" it gave shape to, so did the poemetrical grid pattern units imposed on poetic discourse. This is of very great importance, since it contrasts with the qualitative verse poets of the Middle Ages, who used no single abstract repeatable pattern. They had a number of possibilities, but these cannot be called a pattern in the quantitative sense. For the qualitative kind of poet, then, there could be no split between metre and rhythm. But for the new poets of the Renaissance, such as Shakespeare in the sonnets, there was a split between metre and rhythm. Being a perfect mental concept, a production of the human mind, metre (like geometry) could be applied instrumentally from the outside as a means of control. In this it resembled the mathematics of emergent science that were being developed in the late sixteenth century.

Science and the Lyric

Science and Painting and Literature are supposed to be very different enterprises. And so they are on all but the most crucial and suppressed levels of activity as discourse. For they all constitute "reality" in their different ways, but from a common base inside society. In the key period, the Renaissance, science sought to be objective and to use underdetermined discourse, while the lyric used overdetermined discourse and approached the world subjectively. The two join together, however, in the way that each reproduces the unified ego. Science aimed for a straight subject/object split with the subject "I" as an observer of objective nature, who was seeking out or imposing order on nature. The lyric gives shape to emotions by controlling them, thus to help create the unified "I" from the other side to that of science. Both emanate from the same unified bourgeois "I" that the two discourses have helped to reproduce down to the twentieth century.

After 1910 and All That

We can best see the state to which the iamb and British poetry had been reduced in La Belle Epoch by comparing a typical few lines from "The Fires of God" by John Drinkwater, in *Georgian Poetry 1911-12* (published 1912 in London) to the first fourteen lines from Eliot's "Prufrock" poem (see p. 39), written in the United States in 1911 (published 1915 in London).

> Time gathers to my name;
> Along the ways wheredown my feet have passed
> I see the years with little triumph crowned,
> Exulting not for perils dared, downcast
> And weary eyed and desolate for shame
> Of having been unstirred of all the sound
> Of the deep music of the men that moved
> Through the world's days in suffering and loved.

Here the six syllables of the first line (which is really a second title) give way to seven other lines of exactly ten syllables each. These iambic pentameter lines get some relief from a few rhythmic variations: the spondee (/ /) in the first foot of line one "Tíme gáthers"; the spondee at the end of líne thrée "dówncást"; the pyrrhic (◡◡) at the beginning of line seven with "Of thé", followed by the spondee "déep músic"; and the pyrrhic and spondee in the first two feet of the last line "Through the wórld's dáys". The first three line units confine semantic and syntactical meaning within their boundaries, while four, five, six, and seven run syntactic and semantic meaning over the line unit boundaries. The poem has an ordered abcbacdd rhyme scheme of well-worn rhyme words from a rhyming dictionary. They lack freshness: name/shame; passed/cast; crowned/sound; moved/loved (this latter breaking finally the predictability). Its language tends to the archaic ("wheredown") and reaches cliché ("triumph crowned", "weary eyed"), and the last lines seem to get somewhat lost amid the music and marching metaphors. In fact, this poem limps and whimpers out the passive life which serves as the theme of this lament for a wasted life. It reverses the old saying that "A rolling stone gathers no moss" by having a passive, static name worked over by the active abstraction "Time" which puts the moss on the name. A poem typical of Georgian poetry, it sits on the margins of a bustling world of change in which it cannot participate. The voice—that of one at the heart of the largest Empire the world had ever seen—knows the Empire game is up. The poetry does not reflect an authentic act of poetic construction discoursing on weariness, but rather pours worn-out feeling into worn-out pre-existent form to reveal the bankruptcy of the British liberal intelligentsia just before World War I.

We can see the difference immediately in T.S. Eliot's "The Love Song of J. Alfred Prufrock" (see p. 39), a poem written in the bustling, burgeoning new empire to be: the United States. The poem grasps the very passive character typified in the Drinkwater poem as its subject and theme, and, on the level of both material signifier and conceptual signified, wrings its neck. In violent contrast to the Drinkwater poem, Eliot's work has the great virtue of acting out in its material form the immense vitality of the times in which the poem was written. This vitality energizes the whole poem and becomes the poetic frame or context that defines its opposite, the defeated liberal bourgeois ego which is Prufrock. It represents the forces of a new age, the antithesis to the thesis which was the unified ego.

The first fourteen lines from the Prufrock poem have widely varied lengths, ranging from the opening line's seven syllables through the line lengths 12, 12, 11, 6, 10, 10, 12, 7, 10, 7, 8, 9, 7. Eliot uses rhyme, but only partly in the traditional fashion. He sets out with a conventional rhyme theme "I/sky" to set up some standard expectations. Then he disrupts these expectations beginning in line three with "table". We ask as we always ask about rhyme: what will the rhyme word be? Able? Fable? But Eliot completely disrupts traditional expectations by not providing a rhyme word, even though the next two lines (streets/retreats) suggest that a rhyme word will be forthcoming. He does the same thing in line 10 with "question", which not only leaves us hanging on for the rhyme that never arrives, but suspends us semantically because we never do learn what the question might have been.

So much, then, for the attack on rhyme from within rhyme. Eliot goes on to do the same thing with rhythm. The three ten-syllable lines (lines 6, 7, 10), which have the iambic pentameter rhythm of the Drinkwater poem, serve as the target lines for this attack. The other lines dash into a virtuoso pyrotechnical performance to bombard us with a barrage of spondees, trochees, pyrrhics, and cretics. At the time of publication this practice appeared obscene or barbaric to the shocked, iambic structured mind (and still does). And so did the scandalous imagery, those low-life metaphors and similes which still buzz with energy in relation to the world-weary weight of the Drinkwater lament.

As Marshall McLuhan said: "the medium is the message". That certainly proves to be true in both of these poems. Their medium-messages reverberate on many levels. Most importantly, Eliot does not adopt the voice of an English gentleman (which he later became), but asserts the aggressive fervour of a former colony. This self-confident colonial voice asserts itself in the heart of the British Empire, whose power in the world it would soon inherit. The first message of this medium comes as the bad news from the colonies that the mother country had better move over, for it will no longer control the cultural hegemony of the English-speaking world. The second message announces the end of the unified ego of the English gentleman in the modern world. Moreover, the medium-message continues, the iambic grid which held the unified ego together can no longer satisfy the expressive needs of a "modern" age filled with unprecedented experiences. At best, iambics could be but one possibility among many. This connection between poetic medium and actual character we know from the critical pronouncements of Eliot, Pound and others, all of whom railed against the notion of "personality". These revolutionaries plotted from on the far right of the political spectrum, and set out to assassinate—on the level of high culture—the unified ego of the liberal gentleman as represented by the Drinkwater poem, that lament by a weak, scarcely alive, unified ego. The very disruptive and fragmented form of the Eliot poem, then, represents the fragmented modern ego in its passive form and society in its active form. In this it foresees the rise of big government and the dominance of big government over the individual. One of the great ironies of our century is the fact that these right-wing radicals blasted a way through the privileged discourse of the old establishment and made way for a poetics with very definite democratic possibilities.

An Earlier Attack

The attack on quantitative metre had begun earlier from within England by the Jesuit priest Gerard Manley Hopkins. Hopkins developed some radical leftist views as a result of the human squalor which he witnessed when serving his order in a working class district of the port city of Liverpool. In a life that oscillated between acute depression and joyous celebration of the materiality of the physical world, the sensitive Hopkins—well educated and well aware of the ideological underpinnings of the iamb—developed his own form of the old qualitative metre, which he called "sprung rhythm". He did not, however, go all the way and discard rhyme as well. Born in 1844 in Highgate, London, where Marx was to be buried, Hopkins died in 1889. His poems were not published until 1917, after the appearance of Eliot's "Prufrock", and after the bankruptcy of the old ruling elite had been made abundantly clear on the battlefields of France in the midst of World War I.

Modernism, Democracy, and the Colonies

The revolution of modernism opened the way for the American voice to come fully out from under its feeling of cultural inferiority with respect to the English Canon, the Literature of the imperial centre. This event ultimately led to the emergence of the same desire in other former white British colonies such as Canada and Australia.

More on Quantitative Metre: Types

Along with the iambic metre imported from the Greeks, precociously by Chaucer (d. 1400) and definitively by the court poets of Henry VIII, came other metres:

ᴗ /	iambus (iambric)
/ ᴗ	trochee (trochaic)
ᴗ ᴗ	pyrrhic (pyrrhic)
/ /	spondee (spondaic)
ᴗ ᴗ /	anapest (anapestic)
/ ᴗ ᴗ	dactyl (dactylic)
ᴗ / ᴗ	amphibrach
/ ᴗ /	cretic
/ / /	mollossus
ᴗ ᴗ ᴗ	tribrach
ᴗ / / /	epitrate
/ ᴗ ᴗ /	choriambus
ᴗ ᴗ / ᴗ	ionic minor
/ / ᴗ ᴗ	ionic major
/ ᴗ ᴗ ᴗ	paeon

A metrical foot in Renaissance and post-Renaissance English will normally contain either two or three stresses, but feet can slide into each other to produce larger configurations, as we can see in the choriambus / ᴗ ᴗ /, which consists of a trochee / ᴗ followed by an iambus ᴗ /. The names all come from the Greek.

Line in Quantitative Metre

The term "line" originally meant "linen thread", and it still has this association when we speak of ropes as life "lines" (traditionally measured in feet). A poetic line of quantitative rhythm is defined by the number of feet it has, since a "foot" is the atomic (indivisible) unit of the line. Again the names are from the Greek, this time from the Greek signs for numbers:

(1)	monometer	ᴗ /
(2)	dimeter	ᴗ / ᴗ /
(3)	trimeter	ᴗ / ᴗ / ᴗ /
(4)	tetrameter	ᴗ / ᴗ / ᴗ / ᴗ /
(5)	pentameter	ᴗ / ᴗ / ᴗ / ᴗ / ᴗ /
(6)	hexameter	ᴗ / ᴗ / ᴗ / ᴗ / ᴗ / ᴗ /
(7)	heptameter	ᴗ / ᴗ / ᴗ / ᴗ / ᴗ / ᴗ / ᴗ /
(8)	octameter	ᴗ / ᴗ / ᴗ / ᴗ / ᴗ / ᴗ / ᴗ / ᴗ /

Rhythmic Variations

We can see the iambic norm in the following line from Keats' "Hyperion":

$$\cup \; / \quad \cup \; / \quad \cup \; / \quad \cup \quad / \quad \cup \quad /$$
My life / is but / the life / of winds / and tides

We find a spondee in this line from Shelley:

$$\cup \; / \quad / \quad / \quad \cup \quad / \quad \cup \quad /$$
I found / Him not / in world / or sun

The spondee stresses "Him" and cooperates with the upper case "H" to produce a foregrounding for the pronoun which places great emphasis on the sign.

Variation works in a number of ways in this line from Tennyson:

$$/ \quad / \quad \cup \; / \quad / \quad / \quad \cup \; /$$
Ring out / the old, / ring in / the new

Tennyson's iambic tetrameter line has mid-line juncture or caesura which splits the line in half to foreground and connect the repeated spondees while suggesting the slow reverberations of a big bell.

The Keats line

$$\cup \; / \quad \cup \quad / \quad \cup \; / \quad / \quad / \quad \cup \quad /$$
For I / have seen / my sons / most un / like Gods

foregrounds "most" to supercharge its conceptual meaning; and this line from Meredith has two spondees:

$$/ \quad / \quad / \quad / \quad \cup \; / \quad \cup \quad / \quad \cup \; /$$
And now / Love sang; / but his / was such / a song

Here the two spondees create a dramatic effect which foregrounds both the deictic of time "now", and the personification of "Love" (aided by the upper case letter).

A choriambus works to good effect in this line from Arnold:

$$/ \quad \cup \quad \cup \; / \quad \cup \quad / \quad \cup \; / \quad \cup \quad /$$
Thou through the fields // and through / the woods / dost stray

The line divides in two with the first sweeping part of the choriambus suggesting the ease of walking through open fields, while the second suggests the relative difficulty of moving through trees in the woods. Speaking of the lights of France seen from England, Arnold uses the paeon to act out the effect of lights appearing and disappearing through the foregrounding and backgrounding rhythmic stresses:

$$/ \quad \smile \smile \ /$$
Gleams and is gone

The backgrounding action of two soft stresses can create other results as we see in this line from Keats:

$$/ \ \smile \quad \smile \ / \quad / \quad / \quad \smile \ / \quad / \quad /$$
Just at the self / same beat / of Time's / wide wings

Aided by the alliteration of the ''s'' phonemes, the background soft stresses ''at the'' in the choriambus make the following three hard stresses insistently beat out the conceptual meaning of these signs through the material signifiers in a full four-degree stress, which contrasts with the three-degree stresses of ''Time's wide wings''.

We find a pyrrhic foot in this Tennyson line:

$$\smile / \quad \smile \quad / \quad \smile / \quad \smile \smile \quad / \smile \quad /$$
My life / has crept / so long / on a / broken wing

The two short stresses of the pyrrhic, in relation to the iambic that precedes and the cretic that follows, creates an erratic effect to simulate, on the level of the material signifiers, the erratic movement of a bird limping along with a broken wing.

Line

LINE seems a simple enough term, so habituated are we to it, but this sign turns out to be as problematical as any other key term when we examine it closely. "Line" comes from the Latin *linea*, a linen thread. An excellent treatment of "line" by a master disrupter of lines will be found in "Some Thoughts on Line Breaks" by Dennis Cooley, in *Trace* (ed. Birk Sproxton); and in the journal *Open Letter*, under the title "Breaking and Entering".

Let us take at random what most people, inside and outside the academies, would consider to be natural examples of the poetic line. These two are from Traherne, written in the mid-seventeenth century:

> How like an angel came I down!
> How bright are all things here!

The assumption that we have here "natural" line units errs on at least two major counts:

a)   There are no "lines" in nature. "Lines" are semantic and syntactical units, signifiers used by a culture for the purpose of signification inside a semiotic system. This semiotic system exists independently of nature. However, as a mediating system, it is through the signs that we will constitute our understanding of nature and of society inside the textual world of discourse. "Line" is a signifier which signifies an abstract mental concept of a series of point units. A "line" generally has a beginning, a middle, and an end, but has no necessary length (e.g. tow line, pipe line), and no particular direction, for it can go up, down, around, and about.

b)   The judgment that the Traherne lines above are natural poetic lines arises out of a misplaced metonymy, which takes a misplaced part, "these lines", for the whole potentiality of a poetic line. The notion that these are "natural" poetic lines hides an asumption that "traditional" lines with a clean left margin and a pattern of quantitative rhythmic feet can and do represent all the possibilities for a "natural" poetic line. This standard but erroneous notion about "line" comes to us from the sixteenth century, through that century's emerging print culture, and it is one that has been severely questioned in practice by some very serious twentieth-century poets.

Origins of the Renaissance Line (16th c.)

The idea of the line, in the Renaissance sense above, arises out of a number of different but interconnected cultural developments:

a)   the Anglo-Saxon (Germanic) convention of writing and reading from left to right, reinforced by the classical Greek and Latin tradition (remembering that very few people read at all until the Renaissance and afterwards);

b)   the development of the Anglo-Saxon language from a synthetic language, where sign positions in a sequence were not so crucial, into an analytical language, of the subject-verb-object linear variety, where position became crucial;

c)   the development of clock time (the quantification of time);

d)   the development of quantitative metre/rhythm related to the development of clock time;

e)   the development in chirography of the habit of clean left margins (Gk. *cheir*=hand; hand-written books);

f)   the disappearance of chirographic culture with its paucity of books, and the replacement of it in the Renaissance by a printed book culture with a new intelligentsia (the oral culture continuing among the mass of the people);

g)   the development of the printed book culture coupled with the notion of individual privacy, starting with private bedrooms with doors, private study space, libraries, and silent (i.e. private) reading;

h) the sensory shift from the privileging of sound in oral feudal culture, to that of sight (the book, landscape painting, etc.);

i) the subject-object split which made the individual subject an observer of nature as object, rather than a participant in nature, in the manner of feudal society and post-modern physics;

j) the beginnings, in the Renaissance, of the elaborated linguistic code with its preference for linear syntax and denotation of language, along with the essay form. This elaborated linguistic code would separate the bourgeois from the mass of the people, who lived within, and still live within, the restricted oral linguistic code;

k) the development of the notion—with the arrival of the elaborated linguistic code—that conceptual meaning is the only meaning worth considering, a view that required the suppression of any sense of the materiality of language;

l) the development of clean new typefaces which made reading easier and faster;

m) the development of the idea of guided human progress, a linear historical notion which aligned itself with clock time to turn the endless repeated cycles of the clock face into a conceptual straight line forwards;

n) the emergence of the need in the new and larger urban cultures to control volatile passions. A straight line ("the straight and narrow") becomes a model of rationality opposed to the curves of passion.

The concept of "line", then, in the sense that it was arbitrarily developed and maintained without challenge from the Renaissance down to the twentieth century, is visual, straight within a pattern, runs from left to right, has a beginning and an end, and consists of an orderly number of atomic unit feet defined by silences, which control in different degrees its forward movement. "Line", thus defined, is a principle of social and psychological control, an ideology, and not a "natural form of poetic discourse".

The Line and Nature

As we saw above, the Renaissance cartographers (map makers) placed conceptual, semiotic grid patterns on the conceptual globe, while the Renaissance painters placed conceptual semiotic grid patterns of geometry on two-dimensional plane sufaces of their canvasses as grid patterns to teach us to look at nature through the controlling screens of geometry. It thus made the single observer, occupying the single privileged "point of view" the most important subject of its craft. Indeed, in a sense, the "subject" of all perspectival representation is not the arbitrary illusion created by the "art object", but the privileged observer of that object. And the Renaissance poets put the screens of geometric line and quantitative metre on language as a semiotic grid pattern to create a similar new discourse of poetry.

Poetic Line and Plain Prose

The poetic line as it evolved in the Renaissance is involved in the same exercise of imposing rational control on discourse as the newly developed plain prose non-fiction of the same historical period. The forms of discourse differ, then, essentially only in that poetry advertises its literariness (overdetermined), while the other suppresses its materiality (underdetermined). Both simulate the patterns of the individual speaking voice. Unless this essential difference is understood in the terms described above, it is easy to fall into the common tendency among critics, which is to view the poetic line *as if it were underdetermined discourse* (i.e. not essentially different from prose). This view represses the material signifying system of poetic discourse, and considers such things as metre and alliteration to be merely devices, ornaments, and additions.

Line and the Visual

Line is a visual concept, a mental entity, which sees its object—as in the historically received straight poetic line—in the following abstract terms:

$$\longrightarrow$$

We can therefore represent the following lines

    Sigma presents the social droves
    With him that solitary roves

in the following geometrical way:

Line and Visual Art

Line as visual concept recalls to us the fact that line is a signifier in the semiotic system of visual art. Visual art uses lines to signify its signified objects—persons, things, and processes—as visual concepts. Visual art, however, has not restricted itself conceptually in the highly obvious manner of "traditional" poetry (other than on the question of the invisible lines which connect all of the signs of the representative to the privileged point of view), for it has two basic concepts of the line, the rectilinear, and the curvilinear:

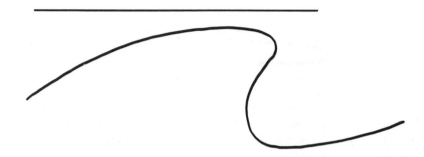

Moreover, visual art has not assumed that line has a single direction, but can send its lines in any direction:

Twentieth-century poetry has reintroduced the curvilinear line into poetry, as in this line written by Dennis Cooley:

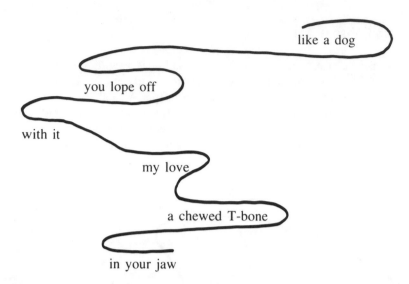

This line obviously curves as it shifts direction.

Twentieth-century poetic projects have generated perhaps three main developments with respect to the old rectilinear line and the new curvilinear line in poetic discourse:

a)   Rectilinear poets such as Frost use the old rectilinear line, but still manage to create subversive work on a semantic level;

b)   Some curvilinear poets see their work as providing a new expressive means that can supplement the old rectilinear forms;

c)   Other curvilinear poets note the cultural presuppositions of control through time and metre, and so on, in the old rectilinear forms, and see that they were one of the means of producing a socially privileged caste with an elaborated linguistic code, a process which had as its more obvious outcome the making of the bourgeois English gentleman. These poets believe that we live in an age which struggles to be democratic and pluralist, that there are more desirable social models than the English gentleman, and that therefore the modern poetic project must be do away with these old ideological practices of privilege. Poetry must be resignified, given new life, such that it can express the age in which we are all now alive. This means a turning away from the elaborated linguistic code, in the direction of the emotionally charged and fragmented restricted code of an oral culture.

The Charged Seme

The modern Cooley poem quoted above consists of a series of charged SEMES, units of semantic meaning, carefully chosen and very carefully placed, despite the arbitrary appearance of the piece. This use of charged semes parallels examples in visual art in the twentieth century where points of tension are created through the interfacing of lines:

———————▶ ◀———————

This gap creates a focal point and a sense of tension. Of course we can find the same sort of thing in the old rectilinear poetry, as in this example from Dryden in the late seventeenth century, but there the charge is contained (we are contained) within the larger controlling structures of rhyme and syntax:

What shall we think! Can people give away

——————————— ———————————

Moreover, reading the Dryden line is more a passive process than an active one, for we dutifully follow the "line" of the argument, the line of the logic, and decode it effortlessly because we are habituated to this kind of discourse. Modern poetic discourse in its extremes has fragmented syntax, removed punctuation, destroyed the notion of continuous geometrical and horizontal lines running from left to right, and so on. There are perhaps six main reasons for this:

a)   this practice foregrounds the material signifying system, to draw attention to its own material base;

b)   this practice attacks and subverts the elaborated linguistic code of the privileged (and those who use it);

c)   this practice takes as its model the restricted code of oral culture, though its vocabulary can go further than the restricted code commonly does;

d)   this practice forces the reader out of the quasi-passive process of reading rectilinear arguments or descriptions, and compels active participation, for the reader must determine which charged seme fits which other charged seme;

e)   the competent modern reader reads at a pace that would simply bewilder readers in the past, a speed which allows him (as Jameson says in *The Political Unconscious*) to hurry him past his own preconceptions. The scattered form of the modern poem of charged semes and rectilinear or curvilinear development forces the reader to think, to make decisions in a slower, more careful and thoughtful participatory process;

f)   Dryden simply assumed the subject/object split of the seventeenth century, which saw man as an observer separated from nature. The curvilinear poets work in the world of post-modernist physics, where the individual is a participant in the process of things, not a passive observer.

Rhyme

The Sign Rhyme

The sign "rhyme" has a history involving a confusion between the Anglo-Saxon *rime* (number) and the Greek *rhythmos*, a communion too complex to discuss here.

Phonemes and Graphemes

Because of the finite number of phonemes in any language, repetition of sounds is inevitable at some point. Rhyme in its various kinds consists of the FUNCTIONAL repetition of the signifier phonemes, and to a lesser extent graphemes, in strategic places to perform certain semantic and other tasks. Along with the difficult task of rhyming, given the limited number of rhyme words in the language, comes the equally difficult task of preventing rhyme in places where it is not desired, where it might be dysfunctional.

Kinds of Rhyme

For present purposes we shall adapt and extend Leech's approach to rhyme in *A Linguistic Guide to English Poetry*, starting with the three-part consonant/vowel/consonant (c v c) pattern, and using upper case letters to indicate the rhymed elements (e.g. C V C). We use this "ideal" three-part pattern for heuristic purposes only, recalling that the consonant before the vowel may, in fact, be from 0-3 consonants, while the consonant after the vowel may be 0-4 consonants.

a) Alliteration: C v c   Fight/Fur

b) Assonance: c V c   hAte/rAte

c) Consonance: c v C   saT/noT

d) Pararhyme: C v C   HaT/HoT

e) Reverse Rhyme: C V c   GRAIn/GRApe

f) Rhyme (the norm):   c V C   hAIL/mAIL

g) Eye Rhyme: the pair are: c V C = graphemically
                               c v C = phonetically
                               (e.g. wreak/steak)

h) Non-Eye Rhyme: the pair are: C v c = graphemically
                                  C V c = phonetically
                                  (e.g. the reverse rhyme
                                  GRApe/GREAt)

i) Historical Rhyme: the pair are: c V C = graphemically
                                     c v C = phonetically (now)
                                     c V C = phonetically (was
                                     in Renaissance)
                                     (e.g. moves/loves)

j) Apocopated Rhyme: (Gk.   c V C = pelf
    apocope=a cutting off) as in c V C (c v c) = self(less)
    pelf/selfless, where the ''less'' is cut
    off, discounted:

k) Identical Rhyme: There are two versions of this. One version repeats the phonetically, graphemically, and semantically identical word, as in Edward Lear's:

There was a young man in Iowa
Who exclaimed, "Where on earth shall I stow her!"
Of his sister he spoke, who was felled by an oak
Which abound on the plains of Iowa.

In the second version, the rhyming signs are phonetically identical but may not be graphemically or semantically identical:

peek/peak
male/mail

l) Broken Rhyme: This is where a rhyme word stretches over two lines. The following is a modern variant from Cooley's *Bloody Jack*:

saw:

bones

was

a barn of muscled bones

a bone of blood

Other Rhyme Terms

a) Hackneyed Rhyme: rhyme at the level of cliche, predictable—the sort of thing that now belongs to greeting cards and limericks:

mOON/jUNE
lIFE/strIFE

b) Hudibrastic Rhyme: so named from the poem "Hudibras", a mock epic of the seventeenth century. A deflating, undercutting, humorous rhyme, like the rhyme "ices/crisis" in Eliot's Prufrock poem.

Rhyme and Stress

We find a strong stressed monosyllabic rhyme, which foregrounds that rhyme word, in Pope's "sneer":

$$\cup \quad / \quad \cup \quad / \quad \cup \quad /$$

Great Cibber sate; the proud Parnassian sneer

and a weak final stressed disyllabic rhyme, which backgrounds that rhyme word, in Pope's "garrets":

$$\cup \quad / \cup\cup \quad \cup \quad / \cup$$

From drawing rooms, from colleges, from garrets

Polysyllabic rhyme commonly creates comic results in English. Byron was a master of this, as we see in his deflating lines on Coleridge:

> And turned, without perceiving his condition,
> Like Coleridge, into a metaphysician

Location of Rhyme

Rhyme may be LOCAL or GLOBAL.

Local Rhyme

This rhyme requires the close proximity of rhyming elements, elements which may stretch over one line into another (line itself being a variable in some twentieth-century poetry). In all English poetry, past and present, local rhyme includes alliteration, assonance and consonance. Gerard Manley Hopkins provides a good precocious "twentieth-century" example from the late nineteenth century:

> I caught this morning morning's minion, king
> dom of daylight's dauphin, dapple-dawn-drawn falcon...

Much less often, local rhyme will include the rhyming of a sign within the line with one at the end (called Leonine Rhyme if the rhyme sign is so-called full or perfect rhyme—terms which unjustly privilege this form of rhyme over others—and occurs just before the mid-line juncture in the couplet form).

Assonance, alliteration and consonance help to provide textual cohesion on the level of the signifier system, as well as to foreground the related signs to create semantic effects (see pp. 105-10).

Global Rhyme

Global end-rhyme serves as a pre-existent (once it has been developed) structure of organization, a discipline or control on what can be said, and on the pace at which it can be said. In this sense, global rhyme stands defined by its opposites: pre-Renaissance alliterative practice, Renaissance blank verse (unrhymed iambic pentameter), and later and freer non-iambic pentameter unrhymed forms of the twentieth century. The avant-garde tendency of the twentieth century is against end-rhyme and the tyranny, or challenge, of traditional rhyme control.

A much more rare form of global rhyme is BEGINNING RHYME, which can be found in Lanier's "The Symphony".

Global rhyme links parts into a structure, exercises control, converts time into space, and accomplishes a number of other things, as we shall see below.

Quality of Rhyme

Rhyme establishes a relationship between proximally close or proximally distant signs. Since a sign consists of material signifier and signified concept, rhyme can establish a relationship on the phonetic and graphemic material levels on the one hand, and on the conceptual side of the signifieds on the other (as we saw above, there can be differences between the phonetic and graphemic). There are basically four kinds of relationships between rhyming signs:

a) Accidental Rhyme: The accidental, unintended rhyme can be bad in poetry, but disastrous in the underdetermined discourse of prose non-fiction. This is because accidental rhyme will foreground the medium and turn it momentarily into overdetermined poetry, thus giving the lie to the claims of underdetermined prose non-fiction to transparency and neutrality of medium.

b) Subordinated Rhyme: With subordinated rhyme the connection between the signified concepts is such that it subordinates the material signifiers under their control. This makes us more aware of the conceptual or semantic sense, than we are of the materiality of the language. We find a good example of this in some lines from A. J. M. Smith's "Son and Heir":

> Like press agents the praises of their lamb
> In minds as polite as a mezzanine floor
> They do concoct a brave politic sham
> To ravel the plot, feature the smirking star

Here the conceptual incongruity of "lamb" and "sham" is such as to cause us to background the related signifiers and to ponder the significance of the two concepts (a sudden drop in register between all the associations of "lamb" and "sham" causes the dislocation and subordination).

c)   Unsubordinated Rhyme: Here the signifier dominates the signified, as we find in the Hudibrastic Prufrock rhyme "ices/crisis". These material signifiers so dominate the signifieds that they diminish semantic meaning and remove any serious sense of the concept "crisis" to which the signified refers, an undercutting effect which serves the poem well. An extreme version appears in Lear's verse:

> He has many friends, lay and clerical,
> Old Foss is the name of his cat;
> His body is perfectly spherical,
> He weareth a runcible hat.

d)   Coincidence: With coincidence, both signifier and signified have something like equal value. We see this with the "floor" and "star" near rhyme in the Smith poem above. There, on the level of signifier, the near vowel phonemes "r" flow mellifluously, while the conceptual connection between earth and heavens produces semantic meaning without disturbing us.

Rhyme as Integrating Principle

> Let others far from foreign grandeurs roam,
> Dearer to me the loneliness of home

In this 1859 poem by Kirby, the two c V C patterns of the rhyme signs exercise rigid control over the forward movement of the couplet. This form exercises a very narrowly rational and authoritarian control over emotion, exactly as we would expect from a Tory mind after the Ontario "red" rebellion of 1837. "Roam" as verb and "home" as noun connect conceptually as conventional opposites. Because of this conventionality we find a coincidence of signifier/signified levels.

The Shakespeare sonnet which follows is freer than Kirby's couplet, but still under tight control, for we can feel these signs clicking into place:

> When to the sessions of sweet silent thought
> I summon up remembrance of things past,
> And sigh the lack of many a thing I sought,
> And with old woes new wail my dear time's waste:

100

With "thought/sought" (a metonym of the first three lines) we have a c V C normative rhyme and a coincidence of signifier/signified. This is because the signifiers do not draw undue attention to themselves, while the signified concepts are compatible.

With "past/waste" we have historical rhyme. These signs used to rhyme c V C, but have now become c v C, the shift in pronunciation being brought about by changes in the language. The gap produced by the split between graphemic and phonetic forms tends to foreground the material signifiers. So powerful, however, is the conceptual or semantic meaning of the signifieds, through which the "past" becomes associated with "waste", that the signifieds subordinate the signifiers.

The rhyme examples above from Lear and Byron, "clerical/spherical" and "condition/metaphysician", most obviously reveal insubordinate signifiers subordinating signified concepts in a way that foregrounds the poetic medium to humorous effect.

Rhyme as Closure

The couplet form, except with open couplets, obviously forces closure on each atomic unit of thought, as we see in these lines from Dryden:

> The kings are slaves to those whom they command,
> And tenants to their people's pleasure stand.

After the three quatrain abab/cdcd/efef development of thought in a Shakespeare sonnet, we get the couplet closure "ee", which can be of several kinds. It can be a rhyme of coincidence, as in

> So long as men can breathe or eyes can see,
> So long lives this, and this gives life to thee.

Clearly this rhyme has a compatibility of the signified concepts (indeed "see/thee" is a metonym of the couplet), and the signifieds are not obtrusive, while the general conclusion is in keeping with the argument of the three quatrains. This is in extreme contrast to the Lear and Byron rhymes we have seen.

In the disyllabic (two-syllable) weak rhyme of the following conclusion, however, the hammering of the signifiers (the rhythmic stress falls on the stop consonant "tt") overcomes the concepts embodied in the signifieds to produce a flippant, rakish conclusion:

> Thus have I had thee as a dream doth flatter:
> In sleep a king, but waking no such matter.

In other Shakespeare sonnets the conclusion does not necessaily follow from the argument of the quatrains.

Rhyme as Play of Signs

As we see with the Shakespeare sonnets above, rhyme may play metonymically to summarize, as parts, the whole of the lines to which they belong. This can go so far as to produce a metonymic narrative sequence, as we see in Shakespeare's "Sonnet 19": Paws, broods, jaws, blood/fleetst, time, sweets, crime/brow, pen, allow, men/wrong, young. One thing we must do, then, when we read a rhymed poem is to scan the right hand margin from top to bottom, for if there is a pattern there, this practice will bring to consciousness what it is that moves us subliminally in any case.

Rhyme, Syntax, and Semantics

Syntax can override rhyme to diminish its restraining effect and produce a more functionally fluid movement which works in tension with restrained end-stopped lines. This tension creates semantic meanings at the subliminal level of experience. A classic example is Yeats' "Leda and the Swan":

> A sudden blow // the great wings beating still
> Above the staggering girl // her thighs caressed
> By the dark webs // her nape caught in his bill
> He holds her helpless breast upon his breast ////

In the fourth line's main clause, the syntax and semantic meaning are contained within the iambic pentameter rhythm of the line to reveal the restraint of rhyme when "breast" turns back to pick up "caressed". The closure (see pp. 110-13) of this line stands in contrast to the first three lines, all of which run on as enjambement to diminish the restraint of the rhymes, but all of which are prevented from moving at too fast a pace by the medial juncture. The effect in these first three lines, then, is one of movement and pauses. Since the first three lines speak on the semantic level of the oscillating violence of rape, and since the last one speaks of (post-coital) inaction or rest, the four lines act out on the material plane of linguistic signifiers the content of the semantic level of the signifieds.

The Yeats lines are yet more subtle. Although "still" of the first line and "caressed" of the second line both run on, they are not of the same quality. Certainly "caressed" simply runs on. "Still", however, is made to oscillate, to run over, and then run back, and then over again, to simulate the effect of beating wings. For "still" is thoroughly, and functionally, ambiguous, having two grammatical levels and at least three semantic ones. Adverbially, "still" could be:

> beating still //
> Above the staggering girl

(continuing to beat);

or

> beating // still
> Above the staggering girl

(remaining above);

but "still" could also be an intransitive verb to indicate motionlessness:

> Beating // still //
> Above the staggering girl

This makes "beating" and "still" an OXYMORON (Gk. *oxys*=sharp; *moros*=dull), a union of opposites. And, of course, a god who has been made flesh is a union of opposites, matter and spirit, even as he is motionless as spirit (eternal, unchanging), and in motion as matter (metamorphic).

It is not that we have to choose one or the other of these meanings. They all work together, with and against rhyme and syntax.

Rhyme, Time, Space, and History

Haber and Hershenson write in *Psychology of Visual Perception* about the wave pattern of eye movements recorded while a Russian was reading a translation of Shakespeare's "Sonnet 73":

> The reader of the sonnet fixates on nearly every word once, with few regressions or refixations. The last word of each line is fixated longer, a pattern probably unique to poetry, and probably representing time used for gaining understanding of the line or checking the rhyme rather than for perception.

We may note about this statement:

a)   it assumes an ideal reader, when there is no such beast. It probably refers to a competent reader, i.e. one who has no physical or psychological impediments and who has also been inscribed with the traditional values and conventions of poetic discourse;

b)   rhyme is not unique to poetry for it can occasionally be found in prose on the one hand, and, on the other hand, not all poetry uses rhyme;

c)   the term ''probably'' reveals a degree of caution, but there seems to be no valid reason why a reader would need ''time...for gaining understanding of the line'';

d)   the phrase ''checking the rhyme'' is somewhat unclear, but it is almost certainly incorrect. This is because rhyme itself, in different degrees and different contexts, acts as a checking device to prevent too fast a forward movement;

e)   the phrase ''rather than for perception'' is also unclear, but almost certainly incorrect, for rhyme functions within poetic discourse (where it occurs, that is) to create certain structures of perception. With some readers, so powerful are those structures of perception, so well have they been inscribed with the need for rhyme, they cannot consider anything without rhyme as poetry at all.

Rhyme performs a number of functions, but perhaps the most important of these is that of control of forward movement. Yet there is more than meets the eye in the matter of this forward movement. To understand it we need two concepts from ''Space, Time and Modern Culture'' by David Gross in *TELOS* #50. These are SUPERPOSITION and JUXTAPOSITION. Superposition relates to the linear syntagma in the sentence. Gross writes:

> In a superpositional mode of thought, things are seen to follow one another since the disappearance of something is required for something to replace it; even so, every new entity is viewed as emerging out of a previous state of affairs which in some ways is still contained and perpetuated in what has displaced it. In superpositional thought, then, time is carefully taken into account, and continuity is given priority over contiguity.

We find time and superpositional thought related on two levels in the first line of Shakespeare's ''Sonnet 12'':

When I do count the clock that tells the time

Here the linear superposition of sign after sign speaks of time and clocks on the level of the signified concepts. But so well has Shakespeare internalized the notion of time, he makes his string of signifiers act out the conceptual meaning as iambic pentameter beats, alliteration (count clock, tells time, the that the) and assonance (When tells, I time) combine to make the line "tick". The line is thus contained on the levels of signifier and signified within the concept of time.

What about juxtaposition? Gross defines this as:

> In a juxtaposing mode of thought, things are set next to or alongside one another in a spatial medium that makes time irrelevant.

Superposition belongs to time, then, and juxtaposition to space. One of the key functions of rhyme therefore becomes that of converting time-oriented superpositional thought and linear sign sequences into spatial relations. On a local level in a sequence of signs, a repeated phoneme in alliteration or assonance will collapse the temporal distance of reading between one sound and its repeat into a spatial relation. It does so by coalescing with its other, in very short term sensory memory. In the larger time frame of the whole rhymed poetic text, a rhyme word recalls its other from short term memory to collapse the whole time frame into spatial relations. This is why we feel a spatial unity in the poem.

At this point we can begin to understand one feature that defines the Anglo-Saxon alliterative verse, as distinct from the typical rhymed poem of later times. The alliterative lines on the local level (along with the different grammar) prevent any sense of linearity from developing, for the repeated phonemes in the first and second half of each line keep turning back upon themselves as they meet in sensory memory.

We can also begin to understand what lay behind the work of the poetic revolutionaries in the twentieth century who fragmented syntax and rhythm and attacked the notion of rhyme through their avoidance of it. They were (and are) involved in the same adventure as those engaged in avant-garde physics: in fleeing from naive realist notions of space and time as containers, into an Einsteinian world of a four-dimensional space-time continuum. In this view, time and space are relational categories which have to do with events in process. They are not "things".

Foregrounding

A poem, a structure built up out of various sub-structures, uses binary elements of the signifying system itself as signifying devices to foreground repeated patterns against background normative patterns. We have examined this process with respect to metre and rhythm, where significant variations of rhythm can be foregrounded in relation to the normative repeated unit metre of the background. Commonly repeated patterns of sound which can accomplish similiar effects include alliteration, assonance, consonance, and dissonance.

Alliteration

In contrast to rhythm and metre, where variation occurs against a background of a normative or repeated pattern, alliteration refers to foregrounding by repetition of initial consonant sounds which occur against the background of usually diverse ranges of sounds. As with rhythmic variations, there are reasons why this foregrounding occurs:

a)   it can be accidental because semantic necessity forces the use of two proximally related signs beginning with the same phoneme;

b)   it can be used to provide a sense of order amid the other arbitrary sounds;

c)   it can be employed to foreground two or more signifiers separated by space on the line (and in the time taken in reading) so as to join their signified concepts on the foregrounded semantic level and to stress their conceptual meaning, creating a shorthand semantic recapitulation through the foregrounding act;

d)   it can collapse time into space by collapsing temporally and spatially separated sounds into a single, but local, unified space (see p. 105).

In the Shakespeare line

When I do count the clock that tells the time

"count clock" and "tells time" neatly summarize the semantic meaning of the line foregrounded by the repeated material signifiers. Here, in fact, we have lurking remnants of the Old English four stress line. We can see buried in the iambic pentameter rhythm:

$$
\begin{array}{ccccc}
/ & / & / & / & / \\
\end{array}
$$

When I do count the clock that tells the time

$$
\begin{array}{ccccc}
1 & 2 & 3 & 4 & 5 \\
\end{array}
$$

the alliteration:

When I do count the clock that tells the time
$$
\begin{array}{cccc}
1 & 2 & 3 & 4 \\
\end{array}
$$

106

an enactment of the ideological war at the level of old and new rhythmic systems.

Assonance

Assonance refers to the repetition of identical vowel sounds in close proximity to each other, and these, too, involve an interaction between space and time to produce a unified foregrounding, shorthand effect. We see this in Sir Charles G. D. Roberts' sonnet "Burnt Lands":

> On other fields and other scenes the morn
> Laughs from her blue—but not such fields are these,
> Where comes no cheer of summer leaves and bees
> And no shade mitigates the day's white scorn.

Assonance foregrounds:

> fields   scenes
> but such   fields these
> leaves   bees
> shade   mitigates   days

The signs "fields" and "scenes" summarize the pastoral state of nature elsewhere, scenes suggesting something positive. The disjunctive "but" joins "such" phonetically. At this foreground level, "such" grammatically joins "fields", which through assonance links with "these" to provide a polar contrast between there and here.

The "leaves and bees" we can perhaps best deal with under Onomatopoeia (see below), but the assonance of "shade mitigates days" speaks in positive terms of what has been negated by the "no" in the line. This technique, available only through foregrounding, sets up brilliantly at the level of the material form of the poem, the abstract thesis: namely, that nature perpetually renews itself. "Shade mitigates the day's white scorn" enters into a dialectical situation with its opposite, and foregrounded, "mitigates" to suggest the promise of what will again be.

Internal Near Rhyme

The lines from Roberts' "Burnt Lands" provide a good illustration of the way in which INTERNAL NEAR RHYME foregrounds over the space of more than one line:

fiel<u>ds</u> scen<u>es</u>
fiel<u>ds</u> th<u>ese</u>
fiel<u>ds</u> b<u>ees</u>

Consonance

We can see this foregrounding technique operate over a considerable distance in a poem by W. D. Valgardson:

> You are choking
> On a lump of old age.
> Shipwrecked in a house of fading photographs,
> Footstools, and windows crammed with geraniums,
> You cling desperately to the arms of your leather chair,
> Gauge the wind, hours of sunshine, measure the seconds
> By the slow tripping of your heart...

In this poem we see consonance linking and foregrounding a<u>ge</u>, <u>ge</u>raniums, <u>Gauge</u>; and cho<u>king</u>, shipwre<u>ck</u>ed, <u>cl</u>ing. Consonance mixes in with other elements to link geranium<u>s</u>, arm<u>s</u>, mea<u>s</u>ure, second<u>s</u>.

Onomatopoeia

The original meaning of this word (Gk. *onomatopoia* = the making of words) adopts the philosophical view, common to the ancients, that there was a connection between the physical language (material signifiers) and the thing a sign refers to. This is not a modern view of language.

The *Oxford English Dictionary* defines "onomatopoeia" as "The formation of a name or word by imitation of the sound associated with the thing or action designated." The phrase "<u>leaves</u> and b<u>ees</u>" in Roberts' "Burnt Lands" creates, through the long vowel sounds, the assonance, the hard stresses and the terminal hard "z" sounds, the general effect of a buzzing bee, and since the poem is about nature as process, the "leaves" (which do not buzz in nature) are made to buzz as if in echo of the bees, to stress the symbiotic relationship between leaves and bees.

Cohesion and Coherence

As Jerry R. Hobbs writes in *Towards an Understanding of Coherence in Discourse*: "When coherence is present in a discourse, it is almost invisible. By contrast, when a text lacks coherence, this lack is perhaps the most striking feature of the text." He proceeds "Coherence isn't Cohesion." To be sure, "In standard usage, 'cohesive' and 'coherent' can be used interchangeably. Both mean 'hanging together'." But cohesion is used in linguistics (Halliday and Hasan, *Cohesion in English*) to refer to the way sentences hold together:

SMITH went down the street. HE was going to the store. [emphasis mine]

The "He" here links cataphorically (backwards) with its reference unit "Smith", since going to the (textual) store sounds like a plausible enough reason in a textual world for walking down the (textual) street. These two clauses therefore exhibit cohesion, because they hang together. They also have coherence because the fused signifieds or concepts are compatible. Consider the following, however:

SMITH walked down the street. HE didn't like Italians. [emphasis mine]

These two clauses have signifier cohesion, but not signified or semantic coherence. While the clauses hang together as syntactic and grammatical sequences through the cataphoric linkage, the signified concepts are semantically incompatible because they do not belong to the same, or even remotely related, classes of experience. Each clause makes sense semantically as a separate utterance, but together they do not. They therefore do not have coherence.

Consider the following poetic lines: the first example is Shakespeare's "Sonnet 30" from the very late 1590s, and the second is the first fourteen lines of T.S. Eliot's "The Love Song of J. Alfred Prufrock" from the second decade of the twentieth century:

When to the sessions of sweet silent thought
I summon up remembrance of things past
And sigh the lack of many a thing I sought
And with old woes new wail my dear times waste.
Then can I drown an eye unused to flow
For friends hid in death's dateless night
And weep afresh loves long since cancelled woe
And moan the expense of many a vanished sight
Then can I grieve at grievances foregone
And heavily from woe to woe tell oer
The sad account of forebemoaned moan
Which I new pay as if not paid before.
  But if awhile I think on thee dear friend
  All sorrows are restored and sorrows end.

Let us go then, you and I,
When the evening is spread out against the sky
Like a patient etherised upon a table
Let us go through certain half-deserted streets
The muttering retreats of one night cheap hotels
And sawdust restaurants with oyster shells
Streets that follow like a tedious argument
Of insidious intent
To lead you to an overwhelming question
Oh do not ask what is it
Let us go and make our visit

    In the room the women come and go
    Talking of Michelangelo.

The Shakespeare sonnet is a tightly bound sequence held together by the "When...Then...Then..." structure, the rhyme, the ten-syllable iambic lines, and the linear syntactical order of superpositional thought. The Eliot passage, up to the couplet, varies the line length but remains rhythmic: keeps the linear superpositional thought pattern, but strains it with the "different" images. It keeps the beginning of a binding structural cohesion with the repeated "Let us go", but plays with rhyme between straight rhyme (I/sky) to no rhyme (table) to graphemic but not phonetic near rhyme (streets/hotels) to near rhyme (hotels/shells) to, in the couplet, humorous hudibrastic rhyme (go/ Michelangelo). Eliot keeps textual cohesion, then, in the first twelve lines, but strains coherence somewhat. Finally, with the couplet, he breaks coherence entirely, at least in terms of the patterns in the Shakespeare sonnet.

And that is exactly the point: as a modernist in a new and decisively urban age of mass society and alienation, Eliot wants to create the effect of a society which has thrown off the inheritance of the past, the connection between man and nature, and the practice of tightly bound poetic closure (see next section). In short, Eliot retains the elements of linear superpositional thought, over the distance of a number of lines, as in the twelve here, but then disrupts them by juxtaposing the alien couplet and creating a semantic gap. The manner in which he does the disrupting with the hudibrastic rhyme makes the Prufrock text an example of disruptive Menippean discourse (pp. 208-9).

Closure

In her *Poetic Closure: A Study of How Poems End*, Barbara Herrnstein-Smith notes that whether we deal with a painting and its spatial orientation, or poetry with its temporal orientation (by virtue of the time taken to read the line sequences), we meet with CLOSURE, the means of closing an art object system to make us feel it to be "integral: coherent, complete, stable." As to the history of closure, she observes that the rise of techniques to create closure was strong in the English Renaissance, at its maximum in the eighteenth century, much lessened in romantic poetry, and minimal in modern poetry. Herrnstein-Smith sees weak or minimum closure, with a tendency towards anti-closure, as the mark of modern poetry. This shift, she says, indicates a change in attitude towards art, revealing a new view of man and his place in the world, one that does not share the certainties which have been the main characteristic of western culture from the time of the Renaissance to the twentieth century.

Poetry from the Renaissance onwards had a beginning, a middle, and an end, towards which the poem moved, to make any poem teleological (Gk. *telos*=end): i.e. ordered by the poem's movement towards its specific end. We can well see that this poetic discourse particularly reflected the teleological view of history which emerged from the Renaissance. This period created the teleological metanarrative of "progress" (see p. 145) through science and learning. It saw an ideal utopian future where the material and spiritual needs of man would be met in an authentically human and unalienated world.

Closure and Frost's "Stopping by Woods..."

An examination of several elements of Frost's "Stopping by Woods on a Snowy Evening" will reveal how closure operates in the poem. We may use it here as an example. The key technique seems to be the variation of an established pattern.

> Whose woods these are I think I know.
> His house is in the village, though;
> He will not see me stopping here
> To watch his woods fill up with snow.
>
> My little horse must think it queer
> To stop without a farmhouse near
> Between the woods and frozen lake
> The darkest evening of the year.
>
> He gives his harness bells a shake
> To ask if there is some mistake.
> The only other sound's the sweep
> Of easy wind and downy flake.
>
> The woods are lovely, dark, and deep,
> But I have promises to keep,

And miles to go before I sleep,
And miles to go before I sleep.

a) Rhyme: the rhyme pattern proceeds through an incremental first three quatrains to set up a pattern of expectation: abcb / cded / efgf /. The last stanza breaks this pattern with gggg.

b) Infinitive Verbs: this poem sets up a pattern of infinitive verbs which it then varies at the end.

Infinitive		
To watch	1. 4	beginning of the last line of the 1st stanza
To step	1. 6	beginning of 2nd line of 2nd stanza
To ask	1. 10	beginning of 2nd line of 3rd stanza
to keep	1. 14	end of 2nd line of 4th stanza
to go	1. 15	middle of 3rd line of 4th stanza
to go	1. 16	middle of 4th line of 4th stanza

The expected infinitive at the beginning of line 14 in fact appears at the end of that line, and this is the very line where the rhyme should have changed if the incremental pattern were to be continued.

c) Repetition: Frost also breaks the pattern when he repeats line 15:

And miles to go before I sleep,
And miles to go before I sleep.

d) Juncture: Frost's poem proceeds with differing degrees of terminal juncture but no medial juncture, except the slight one in the first line of the third stanza:

The woods are lovely, / dark, and deep //

e) Verb: the alternation of connective and active verbs gets summarized in the final stanza with ''are'' (line 13) and ''have'' (line 14), which later dominate lines 15-16.

f) ''I'' Pronouns: the two ''I'' pronouns in line 1 get repeated in different form at the end of the last two lines:

I sleep,
I sleep.

Anti-Closure

In the dialogical novel, as with some post-modern poetry, there is a tendency towards open-endedness, which means that the material form must come to rest, but the conceptual options remain open.

Focat and Arrest

In "Lines about 'Lines'" (*Language and Literature*, ed. Ronald Carter), John Sinclair speaks of focusing categories (FOCAT), and a particular species of the focat called the ARREST. A simplified explanation follows.

For heuristic (working) purposes we:

a)   accept as a norm the linear sentence with a subject-verb-object syntax;

b)   call anything which impedes this linearity an "arrest";

c)   note that poetry frequently, typically even, arrests linear development—in different ways at different times;

d)   observe that arrests create different kinds of focus to suit different purposes.

The first few lines of Milton's *Paradise Lost* reverse the subject-verb-object of the normative linear sentence, and produce a dislocated syntax in a sign sequence which races towards the main verb "sing":

Of man's first disobedience and the fruit
Of that forbidden tree, whose mortal taste
Brought death into the world and all our woe
With loss of Eden, till one greater man

> Restore us, and regain the blissful seat
> Sing...

The breathless pace of this passage acts out the speed of "the fall" not only on the level of the signified, but on the level of the material signifier system as well. It shifts at the last minute from what might have been a declarative sentence to an imperative, pausing after "sing" briefly to cause a focusing arrest. This arrest focuses on the material medium of the poem to announce the text as a literary construction and, as the next signs "sing/ heavenly muse" indicate, to announce a literary construction of an epic kind.

Alexander Pope did something similar about fifty years later in the early eighteenth century with his mock epic "The Rape of the Lock":

> What dire offense from amorous causes spring //
> What mighty contests rise from trivial things
> I sing... ///

Here, however, the juncture after "spring" arrests the line to focus on the philosophical language of "causes spring". This prepares the way for the undermining rhyme in the delayed next line ("trivial things"). The high seriousness of "I sing" stands in contrast to vulgar or "trivial things" and is undermined by them.

Further on, Pope writes:

> O say what stranger cause, yet unexplored,
> Could make a gentle belle reject a Lord?

The comma pauses on each side of "yet unexplored" arrest and delay the line to focus on the philosophical discourse "stranger cause, yet unexplored", while preparing for the witty undercutting effect of the second line. This arrest works like the delaying pause before a punch-line in a joke.

In Sylvia Plath's lines

> I shall never get you put together entirely,
> Pieced, glued, and properly jointed

the juncture after "entirely", "Pieced" and "glued" arrests the line to cause a focusing on this fragmented centre, which stands in contrast to the smooth flow of the other sign sequences on each side of them, to make the line act out the conceptual meaning of wholeness and pieces.

The juncture after "flies" and "heat" in the following Howard Nemerov line also arrests to make the line act out its conceptual meaning:

115

The flies, feeling the heat, keep on the move

In the Ann Sexton lines

Cinderella and the prince
lived, they say, happily ever after

the arrest caused by the juncture on each side of "they say" gives the lie
to the "commonly held view" conjured for the reader by the phrase.

The Phoric Process

The 1985 Harper Handbook of Literature defines ANAPHORA as:

> The technique of beginning successive clauses, phrases, or lines with the same word: 'The voice of the Lord is powerful. The voice of the Lord is full of mystery. The voice of the Lord breaks the cedars.' (Psalm 29)

We can find much the same definition in Peacham's *The Garden of Eloquence* (1577), and in any one of the hundreds of such handbooks that have been produced since. However, this definition simply will not do. To start with, it does not adequately describe its own example above, which begins in each of the three instances with the same repeated noun phrase. Great developments have occurred in linguistics and computer science in recent times to change our understanding of anaphora, and it is to these that we must turn: these works include such texts as Halliday and Hasan's *Cohesion in English*, and the monograph by Brown University computer specialist Graeme Hirst, ''Anaphora in Natural Language Understanding''.

We must start with some definitions: the ''phora'' comes from the Greek *pherein*, which means ''to carry''. The various prefixes to this word are all from the Greek:

PROCESS	UNIT
endophora (*endo* = within)	endophor
anaphora (*ana* = forward)	anaphor
cataphora (*cata* = backwards)	cataphor
exophora (*exo* = outside)	exophor
homophora (*homos* = the same)	homophor

The "phora" morpheme signifies a linking process, while the "phor" morpheme signifies the semiotic unit, the sign or sequence of signs, through which the process of linking is accomplished.

ENDOPHORA consists of both anaphora and cataphora. It refers to the way in which a certain kind of linking occurs within the textual world. ANAPHORA may be defined as the process in discourse in which the anaphor reaches forth across the space of a linear sequence or sequences of signs to connect with an identical or related target semiotic and semantic reference unit or units. For example, this sentence from Marlyn's *Putzi I Love You You Little Square*:

> SHE ran into the store, closing the living room door behind HER and smiling when SHE saw that it was not a customer but Julien who was standing by the display window. [emphasis mine]

The anaphors "she...her...she" ("her" substitutes to provide variety while maintaining conceptual continuity and identity) lead us a few lines later to the target reference unit "Ellen".

CATAPHORA works in the opposite way, as in this excerpt from Ethel Wilson's *Swamp Angel*:

> Ten twenty fifty brown birds flew past the window and then a few stragglers, out of sight. A fringe of MRS VARDOES'S mind flew after them (what were they?—birds returning in migration, of course) and then was drawn back into the close fabric of HER preoccupations. SHE looked out over the green garden..."
> [emphasis mine]

Here "she" looks back cataphorically to the reference unit "Mrs Vardoe".

EXOPHORA works deictically (a locative device) inside the textual world to carry us outside the textual context, as when a character opens a door and says in response to a question: "Sorry, he is not here." This "he" refers outside the textual context.

HOMOPHORA refers to the definite article "the" in the special sense that distinguishes it from ordinary usage in a string of anaphors "the...the...the...".

By contrast, the homophor refers to the unique (or what is claimed to be unique), as in "the" special car, "the" special beer and so on. It is a favourite of advertisers and hucksters.

The chief characteristics of the "phoric" process may be listed as follows:

a)   it requires at least two related signs or sequences of signs in a larger sequence of signs such as a text, as in these lines from Sinclair Ross' *As For Me and My House*:

> PHILLIP'S been strange and gloomy all week. HE eats nothing...HE stands brooding... [emphasis mine]

The two instances of "He" reach back cataphorically to the reference unit "Phillip".

b)   endophora employs its endophors locally in a sequence or sequences of signs, but in addition to this local level it will also use them globally to reach out from one cluster to another, across a whole text. It thus creates local textual cohesion and cohesion on the scale of larger global structures;

c)   notwithstanding the common literary definition, endophora may include more than one sign (e.g. she...her...she), and the endophors may or may not be at the beginning of sequences of signs as we see in the Shakespeare sonnet:

> L1   That time of year thou mayst IN ME behold
> L5   IN ME thou seest the twilight of such day
> L9   IN ME thou seest the glowing of such fire [emphasis mine]

The repeated "thou seest" sets up another endophor, of course. Endophora serves a number of useful functions in a text. These include:

i) it establishes the ontological presence of persons, places, events, and things in the textual world. For example, "I came, I saw, I conquered" not only speaks of action, but the repeated "I" firmly establishes the presence of a specific identity in the text;

ii) it provides textual cohesion;

iii) it helps to thematize the problematic (p. 38);

iv) it helps generate reader interest by withholding information from the reader (a proleptic function). Thus, we do not learn who the "he" of the first chapter is in Dickens' *Hard Times* until the beginning of the second chapter;

v) endophora can be used to foreground the signifier system in a text, as we shall see with the following example from the beginning of Chapter Two of *Hard Times*:

> A man of realities, Thomas Gradgrind, sir. A man of facts and calculations. A man who proceeds upon the principle that two and two are four, and nothing over, and who is not to be talked into allowing anything over. Thomas Gradgrind, sir,—peremptorily Thomas—Thomas Gradgrind. With a rule and a pair of scales, and the multiplication table always in his pocket....

The first "Thomas Gradgrind" reaches back cataphorically through all the endophors in the first chapter and also works amid this local cluster of endophors here.

This brief study of the phoric process indicates how the new computer technologies are deepening our understanding of how discourse works. At the same time they make clear the impoverished character of definitions of literary terms found in the standard dictionaries. Nearly all of these definitions require serious re-thinking.

Markers

MARKERS are the linguistic means whereby we recognize things social and their corresponding linguistic levels. These levels occur within any established or even changing social hierarchy, and require a consideration of the period or place in which a literary text was produced or is set. For example, one of the purposes or functions of the following refrain from the textual world of Eliot's "Prufrock" poem

> In the room the women come and go
> Talking of Michelangelo.

is to "mark" the women and setting as Bloomsbury bourgeois intellectual. Women in the majority culture of the restricted linguistic code do not come and go talking of Michelangelo. Indeed, it is the absence of bourgeois markers in the textual world of Pinter's *The Birthday Party*, and the presence of such markers as "cornflakes" and the restricted code answers, "nice", which mark Meg and Petey as ordinary declining petty bourgeois or borderline working class. The sign "women", of course, is a sex code marker, as are the names "Meg" and "Petey".

We can find interesting things happening through markers in Robert Kroetsch's novel, *Alibi*. The key markers there indicate the ability of Dorf, the protagonist, to shift between the elaborated and restricted codes, a characteristic that Dorf, in the textual world, shares with both Kroetsch and the main line of Canadian prairie-born intellectuals in the empirical world.

The first sentence of the novel reads:

> Most men, I suppose, are secretly pleased to learn their wives have
> taken lovers; I am able now to confess I was.

The passage has the cool measured pace of a sentence dominated by syntagma and denotation, superpositional prose, and it moves forward accordingly in a linear and unobtrusive way. To be sure, "taken" is a metaphor, but it would be sufficiently dead to most rational minds (not to the unconscious, we may suppose) so as not to afford any paradigmatic diversions from the main line of the prose forwards. Yet even so, this passage subtly announces its literariness (itself a form of marking) through rhythm:

/ / ∪∪ / ∪ /∪∪ /
Most men, I suppose, are secretly pleased

∪ / ∪ / ∪ /∪ /∪
to learn their wives have taken lovers;

∪∪ /∪ / ∪∪ / / /
I am able now to confess I was.

Moreover, on this level of the signifying system, we can also find devices of phonetic repetition such as alliteration (most men; suppose secretly; learn lovers; wives was;) and assonance (Most suppose; secretly pleased; I wives I, I; taken able; have am; men confess;) and consonance (suppose pleased wives lovers was; learn taken now). These devices, while obviously here, are relatively unobtrusive, and so the announcement by the text "I am literature" happens in muted, but sure, terms. We see how rhythm works in this passage to shift semantic meaning, to state a theme, and to mark Dorf as a double "I": the rhythm backgrounds the first "I" in the last clause (as it had done the "I" at the beginning) and foregrounds the second one to tell us that there are two Dorfs in this text. This causes the clause to become a microcosm of the macrocosmic text, where we find Dorf shifting between the two "I" positions of the elaborated middle class code of precision and restraint, and the lower class restricted code of a non-book majority culture, that mark these two I's.

A far more emphatic and decidedly literary example of the elaborated code appears further on in a humorous incident:

> I, my private parts scalded and unable to touch myself, unable
> to let Karen come near me with a bath towel.

Here also we have devices of repetition (I my private myself; unable unable; touch towel; Karen come, etc.), and the first three syllables can be scanned in one of two ways:

$$/ \smile /$$
I my pri[vate]

$$/ \ / \ /$$
I my pri[vate]

But either way the "I" gets foregrounded. This foregrounding marks two things: a shift from the passive observer of the opening lines to the active "macho" and changing trickster figure, as well as an impending shift from the elaborated to the restricted code that immediately follows with the phatic

Well shit, I said, Shit.

These markers of linguistic or social levels, or the change between levels in the same character or "I", reveal that markers connect with shifters (see next section), because the same "I" shifts between two different linguistic markers of "I", the elaborated and the restricted linguistic codes.

Dorf tells Karen about having sex with the mysterious Julie in the spa waters of Banff. In her reply, Karen almost drops into the restricted code, but corrects herself:

You Rat, Karen said, Tell me more, I like it.

Dorf continues:

The water was the temperature of her body. Thus my whole body...

At this point Karen interjects in what is initially the restricted code:

Jesus Dorf, Karen said. Don't say thus.

Here Kroetsch causes his text to foreground its codes in a meta-commentary. Sex belongs, Karen's objection says, to the body, and the body belongs to the restricted code of face-to-face relations, while the elaborated code has difficulty with sex and the emotions, being designed for precise rational usage. Karen indicates that "thus" belongs to the most formal level of the elaborated code (academic) as a marker of rational discourse, and it has no place in the discourse on sex and physical experience.

Dorf corrects himself:

It was as if all of me...right up to the neck had entered her body, which in turn...

That's better, Karen said.

Shifters

SHIFTERS refers to the signified concepts in personal pronouns and the way in which those concepts slip out from under the signifier pronouns in the course of character role change or growth. We can readily see this slippage in our analysis of the scene with the first person narrator and the old French peasant in *Generals Die In Bed* (see pp. 190-97). There we witness a SHIFT from the speaker's "I", which views the French peasant *other* as an "It", to an "I" which is part of a fully human "we" community in which the other ceases to be other. He becomes a "thou" in one of Martin Buber's authentically human "I-thou" relationships. Similarly, we watch the speaker's private soldier "I" defending itself against the force of social privilege in the form of the Anglican priest. To accept the overtures of the priest and enter into community on his terms would require a shift that would subordinate the soldier's "I" to a position of dependency on the bourgeois rank of the priest.

In "The Lamp at Noon" the "she", Ellen, resists the patriarchal code of her husband Paul because this would require her to shift her democratic "I", placing her in a subordinate position relative to him. Two differently structured social egos shift and change in the conflict until Ross settles the matter by sleight-of-hand monological closure and affirmation of democratic values in a homeorhetic text.

In *The Birthday Party* Pinter gives Meg and Petey rigid and unchanging egos to make them representative of a social class that apparently learns nothing from experience. By contrast, he creates, in Goldberg and McCann, Literary characters in a textual world who are the very extreme embodiment of the principle of the shifter. So much do they shift that we are unable to find a fixed "I" centre at all in these characters. The point about these characters is, of course, that they are Literary characters whose function is to deconstruct the textual world of realist drama that Pinter sets up at the beginning in the form of Meg and Petey. In terms of their external references beyond the text, Goldberg and McCann point in many contradictory directions at many roles, and in this they contrast with the single-dimensioned declining petty bourgeois characters, the shrivelled unified egos that are Meg and Petey.

In Frost's "Stopping by Woods on a Snowy Evening", the "I" of the speaker shifts significantly from that of the socially conditioned "I" who goes about his socially necessary and socially conditioned rounds, to that of an "I" who gets a glimpse in nature of something more whole, complete, than "getting and spending" in life. The "I" then shifts back to the old socially conditioned "I".

In Hemingway's "Hills Like White Elephants", the constant emphasis and play on the neuter pronoun "it" tells us of an I-It relationship between the significantly unnamed "American" and the "young woman". The American treats the woman as an "it", to be used instrumentally, and although he convinces her that all will turn out well with the abortion (which he will significantly not name), the ending of the text is problematic, with the American's "I" unshifted but with hers having moved in his direction.

Irony

IRONY derives from the Greek *eironia*, where it meant "dissimulation" or the deliberate pretence of ignorance. Irony involves two levels or semantic domains: the level of appearance, and the level of the concealed reality.

Greek Comedy

Although we know a great deal about what Aristotle thought concerning Greek tragedy, we know very little about what he thought concerning Greek comedy. There exists plenty of historical evidence that he wrote a treatise on comedy, but the text of that treatise has been lost. What is particularly unfortunate about this loss is that we would know a great deal more about the school of philosophy which Socrates originated, and which passed through Socrates' student Plato to Aristotle, if we could compare Aristotle's remarks on Greek tragedy to those he made on Greek comedy. As it is, we know only that Greek comedy evolved historically from Greek tragedy at precisely the moment when the Greeks began to question the irrevocability of the ties that bound mankind to the forces that rule the natural world (the world of nature, of "physics"), which was the premise on which the fateful, stately and public enactment of Greek tragedy was built. Indeed, Greek tragedy is itself derived from the dramatic presentations of religious rituals, which date from prehistoric time. The central feature of Greek comedy appears to be that the *eiron* feigned ignorance so as to lead the braggart *alazon* into a trap. In this secularized, degraded version of Greek tragedy, the *eiron* played the part of the fates, who in tragedy led the tragic hero (in comedy the *alazon*), who had usually committed, through some form of blindness and/or hubris, to his or her inevitable doom.

Socratic Irony

Socrates often feigned ignorance in order to trick a student (or an adversary) in dialogue. The "Socratic method", in fact, consists of taking the same position on a so-called "self evident truth", as one's adversary in a dialogue, verifying this sham agreement with one's now overconfident adversary, and then proceeding, by a series of logical deductions from that "self evident truth", to a point which is a logically absurd (and therefore untenable) extension of that "self evident truth". This logically absurd extension, by its very absurdity, calls the "self evidence" of the original "truth" into question, and allows the victor of the verbal battle to challenge, and ultimately to replace, the original "self evident truth" with one of his own design. (This is, incidentally, the very same method which has been used throughout this book to attack the "self evident truths" which underlie a naive realist reading of any text, whether Literary or not.) The point of all this is, of course, that Socrates could not have applied his "Socratic method" to the creation of a very new, highly successful philosophy, had not the Greeks at precisely this period in their history begun to question seriously the inviolate relation between man and nature, and had Greek comedy not invented the device to attack that fundamental premise of its precursor, Greek tragedy. And herein lies the supreme "irony" of Socrates' achievement. He successfully employed the tools of Greek comedy (the purpose of which was to attack the "high seriousness and truth"—the elaborated code—of tragedy, and to entertain the masses in a restricted code), to instruct his students in the nature of the new world view proposed by this new philosophy. One of the Socratic school's strongest and most relentless of attacks, recorded by Plato, was on poets—this at a time when the most highly respected poets of his age (the most respected because they were considered the most authoritative on the subject of how the world, and mankind in the world, interrelated) were the great tragedians. For this "perversion", the citizens of Athens condemned Socrates to death. Yet only three generations later, under the tutelage of the great systematizer of this new world view, Aristotle, Alexander the Great was to put into practice this new perversion of ancient Truth by conquering, and Hellenizing, the entire known western world.

Irony and Traditional Logic

Traditional either/or logic insists that A cannot be A and not-A at the same time. Irony plays havoc with traditional logic because it proposes A as A and not-A at the same time. Irony is characteristic of western culture because western culture has been in a state of constant revolution, particularly since the late Middle Ages/early Renaissance (i.e., the rebirth of classical knowlege) when the term came into English.

Verbal Irony

In VERBAL IRONY, the semantic meaning of a statement (or statements) proves to be the opposite of what it appears to be. Thus, when we say "nice day" on an obviously cold or rainy day, we are engaging in verbal irony.

Situational Irony

A situation in SITUATIONAL IRONY turns out to be the opposite of what it appears to be. We shall see in Leacock's "The Conjurer's Revenge" below that the conjurer *appears* to be doing a conjuring trick when he smashes his adversary's watch, but in *reality* he is performing a dirty trick and actually smashes the watch.

Dramatic Irony

DRAMATIC IRONY refers to a situation in which readers or viewers know something that participants in an event do not know. In "The Conjurer's Revenge", the title tells us in advance that the Quick Man adversary will not defeat the Conjurer. We know something that the Quick Man does not know, and we await the outcome of events.

Irony of Events

IRONY OF EVENTS relates to dramatic irony and it refers to situations in which the action proves to be the opposite of an actor's intentions. Thus, the Quick Man believes he can defeat the Conjurer but he ends up being defeated and humiliated, the opposite of his intentions.

Social and Historical Irony

Dorothy Livesay has described her 1930s long poem "Day and Night" as a documentary poem, a long poem which deliberately incorporates found materials into a work, but transforms them to suit the needs of the poet and the subject. We find, therefore, a social and historical irony in the title, which reverses the name of the popular song of the day by Cole Porter ("Night and Day / you are the one / only you beneath the moon / and under the sun") in order to reveal the gap between the *illusion* of glamorous Hollywood, and Porter's music, and the grim *reality* of the factory enslavement of the proletariat. She does the same with Lenin's famous pronouncement about the uneven process of revolution being two steps forward and one step back. In order to unveil what she considers to be the backward-moving state of capitalism, Livesay wrote:

> One step forward
> Two steps back
> Shove the lever
> Push it back.

This captures the rhythm of the machines and men as the extension of the machines, machines which produce industrial wealth and human impoverishment simultaneously. The "two steps back" doubly signifies the act of working a machine, and historical regression for the workers.

Cosmic Irony

We find one form of this in an early Livesay short poem:

> I cannot shout out the night—
> Nor its sharp clarity.
>
> The many blinds we draw,
> You and I,
> The many fires we light
> Can never quite obliterate
> The irony of the stars,
> The deliberate moon,
> The unsolved firelites of night.

The poem operates through double signification to produce a concrete setting and action in sequence (night, blinds, fires, stars, etc.), and on a parallel level to reveal the text as allegory. On the one level, night is simply night; on another it is the fact—"unsolved finality"—of death. The cosmic irony arises from the assumption of an objective unchanging universe—"stars", "moon"— which have nothing to say about (and nothing to do with) the changing, very mortal human being.

Irony and the Social Unconscious

Speaking of E. J. (Ned) Pratt's poem "Towards the Last Spike", F. R. Scott responds through his poem "All The Spikes But the Last":

> Where are the coolies in your poem, Ned?
> Where are the thousands from China who swung
>   their picks with bare hands at forty below?

He goes on to compare the *absence* of these workers with the over-*presence* of Donald Smith, Victorian capitalist, who drove the last spike in Pratt's account. Scott points to the illusion of reality here which offers the illusion that Smith single-handedly built the railroad, when in reality the workers did, especially Chinese immigrant labourers. Scott thus points to an irony of situation occasioned by social amnesia.

Irony and Hypocrisy

The first few lines of Arthur Hugh Clough's "The Latest Decalogue" proceed:

> Thou shalt have one God only; who
> Would be at the expense of two?
> No graven images may be
> Worshipped, except the currency:
> Swear not at all; for for thy curse
> Thine enemy is none the worse:

Clough creates a persona which embodies the bourgeois hypocrisy of mid-Victorian England as he saw it. We know the speaker must be solid bourgeois from the elaborated linguistic code in which he speaks, or rather the linguistic codes in which he speaks, for he shifts between the public moral code of the King James Bible, a product of the early seventeenth century, and the elaborated plain prose code associated with the rise of science in the mid-seventeenth century. This latter here becomes the cynical private voice of the modern world which undermines the public moral code descending from the King James Bible.

Clough uses the full resources of overdetermined language in these couplets, as we shall see in the first one:

> Thou shalt have one God only; who
> Would be at the expense of two?

The very following of an imperative by an interrogative itself suggests the possibility of undermining of some sort. Imperatives presuppose authority. We conventionally speak of "authority being questioned", and that is precisely the textual situation here. Rhythm works in the same way. The heavy beats of the first six syllables help create the slow and ponderous character of the utterance, to set it in contrast to the light, skipping and mocking iambic feet which follow. This further helps to undermine the pretensions of authority. The "who" at the end of the first line feels a gravitational pull towards the other seven syllables, and this adds to the heaviness of its beat, causing a slight line end juncture. This pause is the equivalent of the pause before a punch-line in a joke. It momentarily restrains the action before the iambs go racing away to do their disruptive work.

We find the same punch-line technique in the second couplet:

No graven images may be
Worshipped, except in currency;

The sign "except" subverts the universality of the injunction in the original imperative, and the iambic rhythms of the adverbial phrase of which it is a part run away from the heavy spondees "No graven...Worshipped, except the currency...."

The same rhythmic binary opposition characterizes the last couplet:

Swear not at all; for for thy curse
Thine enemy is none the worse;

When the line is rearranged, its power disappears:

for thine enemy is none the worse for thy curse.

The doubling up of the "for for" is the equivalent of the comic double-take leading into the punch-line. The double "for for", a hesitant spondee, also mocks the two solemn spondees in the Imperative, and leads straight into the skipping iambs.

Of course, this is the creation, in the condensed terms of the textual world of this poem, of the double-bind values of the Victorian bourgeois in that period of acquisitive individualism, capital accumulation, and Christian morality. Love thy neighbour, says the publicly accepted moral code of the Bible. But if the bourgeois loved his neighbour truly, then he could not exploit him. Not being able to exploit him, he could not accumulate capital. No capital accumulation meant a descent in class to the unspeakable depths of industrial England, or emigration, a move that did not solve the problem. Capital accumulation by contrast meant a denial of the Nazarene's code, hence the double-bind to which Clough, through his cynical persona, draws attention.

Metacharacter

Character

CHARACTER derives from the Greek verb *charassein*, which means "to engrave" (i.e. to cut socially significant forms into a material). We can connect both human character and literary character with the letters on a typewriter (Identical term: "characters"), through their common source in *charassein*. Moreover, as typewriter characters produce socially significant literary and Literary forms through the engraving pressure of inked metal stamps on blank paper, so does a society engrave characters by inscribing individuals with its values (L. *in*=in; *scribere*=to write; to write into). "Character" in the contemporary sense of human and Literary character acquired its meaning in the seventeenth and eighteenth centuries in the midst of the rise of political parties, the mercantile bourgeois class, the nation-state, the first British Empire, underdetermined prose, and the novel form. The very name "novel" (L. *novus*=new) tells us that something new was happening.

The Social Construction of Reality

Berger and Luckmann (in *The Social Construction of Reality*) write: "Humanness is socio-culturally a variable...there is no human nature in the sense of a biologically fixed sub-stratum." They add: "While it is possible to say that man constructs his own nature, it is more significant to say...simply, that man produces himself''. For ''the world of everyday life is not only taken for granted by the ordinary members of society in the subjectively meaningful conduct of their daily lives. It is a world that originates in their thoughts and actions, and is maintained as real by these.'' But, of course, in daily life we are not free to construct any old world we like. We are born into an already named and ''objectified'' world, and we inherit along with that objectification a semantic order ''within which these [objects] make sense and within which everyday life has meaning for me.'' Literary and human characters have in common the fact of being constructed, which is to say, not only in-scribed, but pre-scribed. This commonality between human and Literary character helps to explain why naive realism constantly confuses Literary character with character in the empirical world.

Naive realism has been aided in its confusion of Literary character with empirical character by the claims of the dominant Literary genre and ideology of the last several centuries: ''realism''. We shall see in the following pages what is right and wrong about the ''realist'' character and text.

Metacharacter

Since character and individualism are social constructs which vary from culture to culture, and from one period to another in Western culture, any Literary character will have behind it the central presuppositions of an age with respect to individuality and character. Ages of great change from the late Middle Ages down to the present will have competing presuppositions and metacharacteristics in their intensely concentrated decades of transition. It will be the purpose of these immediately following pages to define the metacharacter which has dominated our culture and Literature from the Renaissance down to the age of Freud.

How Many Children Had Lady Macbeth?

Many years ago, British Literary critic L.C. Knights wrote what deserved to have been a more lasting and influential article called ''How Many Children Had Lady Macbeth?'' Taking a few quotations from Shakespeare's Macbeth, he asked this question not to answer it, but to interrogate the validity of the question itself. His target was the still rampant BIOGRAPHICAL FALLACY, a naive realist view which confuses the textual world with the empirical world. This fallacy sees Literary characters as living characters. It misses the point that before characters are anything else they are textual constructions shaped by discourse.

Mediated and Immediate Character

The naive realist confusion between Literary and empirical character parallels the naive realist confusion of signs with things. The error in both areas arises out of the assumption of an IMMEDIATE or UNMEDIATED relationship between the Literary discourse form and the empirical world. In fact, the discourse form is a means of MEDIATING that empirical world. A painting, a film, or a long narrative poem, using the same data as a starting point, would produce different results because no MEDIUM can be a transparent or neutral FORM of MEDIATION. There can be no single Truth. Different as results would be through the use of the different media, not one of these texts would be right or wrong (assuming the same level of creative competence).

Individualism and Literary Character

As the concept of individualism has changed over historical time, so too has the concept of character (individual) changed in Literature. In Literature as a whole, the process has not been one of linear progress towards a single realization of ideal character, but rather an accumulation, a sedimentation, of layers of concepts of character, all of which in their essential shape still find use. The polarities in the spectrum of character abstractly relate to developments in society from the feudal period down to the twentieth century, our own world being in the process of redefining character in life as well as in Literature.

Feudal

Raymond Williams observes in *The Long Revolution* that the term "individual" meant "member" in feudal society. This corporate individualism presupposed a hierarchy in which everyone had his "proper" place, a place defined by society. Society itself accorded rights and responsibilities to each of the levels, ranging upward from lowly peasant to exalted king. Medieval physics correspondingly saw nature in the same politically conservative terms: rest was assumed to be the "natural" state of a body, and motion unnatural.

Bourgeois Character

The various phases of the bourgeois revolution gradually eroded some of the feudal hierarchies, using the weapons of science and secular humanism. For the new isolated and acquisitive individualism, the individual defined his own space and place through the acquisition of wealth in the market-place. He had no responsibilities to society in the feudal sense. He was a self-made and self-moving man. Society would be taken care of through a balance of competing interests. The Newtonian cosmological system perfectly represents all of these new assumptions about the "nature" of man (and literally "man" because the system remained patriarchal). In this system of classical mechanics, the "natural" state of bodies is motion, and a body once in motion will continue in motion until something stops it. Moreover, the balance of competing interests, the bourgeois concept of the market-place, gets written into gravitational theory and the ordered motion of the planets. Nature here has ceased to be fallen and sinful.

Flat and Round Character

Newtonianism gets written into the concept of Literary character. In his *Aspects of the Novel*, E. M. Forster writes from within the nineteenth-century value system of traditional liberalism. He accordingly privileges the self-moving, independent and isolated individualism which is the equivalent of a planet in Newton's cosmological system. He divides characters into the FLAT and the ROUND, declaring flat characters to be mere types and the round ones—the self moving individuals—to be authentic individuals. In this bold sweep, Forster resignifies the whole of Literature. He privileges one kind of novel character, and subordinates the rest of Literature to an inferior position. In fact, there are no privileged positions in Literature that can be defended beyond the level of mere assertion by authority. Character is a relational term. The kind of character used will be determined in its main outlines by the form of the discourse universe the character must inhabit.

Naive Realism and the Unified Ego

Traditional liberal values produced the ideology of the unified ego or "I". Realist texts take the unified ego (the equilibrium at the beginning of the text,) set it into conflict over values with other egos to disrupt or disunify it (the disequilibrium in the greater part of the text), then resolve the value conflict with an affirmation of values and monological closure (final equilibrium). This affirms the unity of the ego, and massages the reader of these readerly texts into believing that, despite conflict in the reader's (empirical) world, all will turn out well. The process of reading these texts thus reproduces the ideology of the unified ego in readers, a task well served at the level of "popular" Literature by Harlequin romances. Belief in this ideology glosses over the reality of fragmented modern society, fragmented psyches and bad dreams.

135

Character and Proper Names

In *Canterbury Tales*, Geoffrey Chaucer names his characters in feudal style by their corporate function: Knight, Monk, Prioress, Merchant and so on. In the next hundred or more years, these characters would become Mr Knight, Mrs Prior, Master Merchant, for the name of their function would become a proper name or noun. The shift in naming was central to the ongoing rise of the bourgeoisie in society through developments in politics, economics, law and other areas of life. All this led to more modern notions of individualism, and decidedly modern notions of private property, by contrast with the corporate notions of property in feudal society. The sign "proper" in "proper noun" itself connects with "property" in the new sense through a common ancestor, the Latin *proprius*, which means "one's own". Tigar and Levy observe in their *Law and the Rise of Capitalism*:

> The institution of property in the sense it came to have in bourgeois law posits a person (persona) and a thing (res), joined by the legal norm called property or ownership. Human society is dissolved into isolated individuals, and a world of goods split up into discrete items.

The proper noun (proprius) thus names "one's own" body as "one's own" property (proprius). One becomes property in order to potentially have property. It is not difficult to see where the metaphor of human "worth" came from.

These notions about the cultural presuppositions of character and property inform much of our Literature at a deep structural level. But occasionally they emerge in a text which foregrounds them. This happens in *Wuthering Heights*, as Patricia Parker reveals in "The (Self) Identity in the Literary Text" (in *Identity of the Literary Text*):

> Property and proper name are connected, first, in the figure of Lockwood himself: it is he who owns or masters his own text...and lends his name to the single unifying presence of a narrative which repeatedly calls attention to the importance of proper place, property, propriety, and proper name.

Property—as body and goods—is about boundaries, as Parker indicates:

> Property in the sense of the establishment of boundaries—and the prohibition of trespass based on the laws of private possession— appears as well in the frequency in the novel of images such as windows, thresholds, and gates which mark the boundaries between places, or between inside and out.

Character and Semiosis

Literary characters are constituted in Literary textual worlds out of the semiotic fusion of signs into sequences. These sequences have both local and global textual significance within the defining limits of a discourse or genre.

Hierarchy of Character

Typically, in the novel, short story, play, and long narrative poem there will be a hierarchy of characters which we can place in pyramidal form:

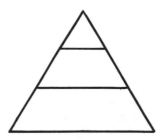

The primary characters at the top will generally be more particularized or more central to the action than those at the lower levels. In Forster's terms these top characters would be round characters. However, centrality to the action and particularization are two very different concepts which work differently in different texts. In Forster's own novels the leading characters are both round and central, while in Fielding's eighteenth-century *Tom Jones* and *Joseph Andrews* the leading characters are equally central, but flat. However, these are also fine novels in which Fielding's flat characters represent an old Tory ideology, in contrast to Forster's characters, who represent nineteenth-century liberalism. On the other hand, the characters Goldberg and McCann in Pinter's play *The Birthday Party* are neither flat nor round (see pp. 187-9).

Most often, the hierarchy of characters in a text will approximate the hierarchies of stratified class or estate society in the empirical world, as we find in anything from Chaucer through Shakespeare to the text of the television show Dallas. In all instances, though, the empirical world is mediated through the discourse.

Discourse Conventions and Generic Code

A writer sets out to produce a particular form of discourse. In the process of doing so he may find that his concept of intended form, say a novel, is too big for his inspiration as that inspiration assumes material shape on paper, or the other way around so that his intended short story must become a novel. In both instances, praxis will require an adjustment of theoretical intentions to the dictations of practice to make the original intentions fit the discourse form, even if the form has to be expanded or developed, in order to *realize* intentions. Since the form of the discourse is the form of the mediation, the generic code becomes the most important of all the codes that go into the making of a Literary text. That is because the GENERIC CODE (see p. 142) sets the limits on what can be done within its framework.

Character and Codes

Within the limits set by the generic code—bearing in mind that a new work may expand these limits—the other codes take their textual shape. Typically, one code will dominate a text. In the medieval play *Everyman* and John Bunyan's novel *Pilgrim's Progress*, religion emerges as the dominant character code: in the first it is feudal Catholicism, in the second it is the religion of a dissenting Protestant sect of the late sevententh century. As the generic name would suggest, in the many psychological realist novels of our age the psychological code dominates.

That a particular code dominates a text does not mean that other codes are absent, even if they cannot be seen. On the contrary, absent codes are mediated through the other codes of the text. We do not have to be told that a character is of a certain rank in society when the dress, food, manners, and housing codes say it in an oblique way.

Narration

Summary: Story, Discourse, Genre, and Text

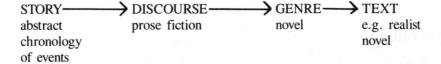

STORY———→ DISCOURSE————→ GENRE——→ TEXT
abstract   prose fiction   novel   e.g. realist
chronology   novel
of events

Tension and Text

The narrative discourse plays over and dislocates the abstract chronological story to develop a creative tension which

a) keeps the attention of the reader;

b) allows the text to move beyond the literal, and often trivial, story;

c) allows the emergence of multiple levels of meaning and a philosophically interesting play with space and time and character.

Analysis and Bracketing

The process of literary analysis is concerned with the relationship between the formal properties of story, discourse, genre, and text. For this reason we initially bracket [the empirical world] for heuristic purposes. Ultimately, however, we will take these brackets off and determine the relationship or relationships between the formal text and the empirical world, noting similarities and differences between a text and other texts, as well as between a text and the structures of the society in which the text emerged.

Modalities of the Text

The three main modalities or ways in which a speaker may use sentences to address someone in English are:

a) DECLARATIVE: "He went away."

b) INTERROGATIVE: "Did he go away?"

c) IMPERATIVE: "[You] Go away!"

And so it is with texts, which may declare, question, command, or do a number of these things at once. A text may be an interrogative text, of course, without having a single question in it. It will, as a whole, question values.

Narrator

a) The author is, first of all, a social individual, not someone who exists somehow separate from society.

b) The social individual who becomes a novelist must also, like his readers, be a reader of novels in order to master the discourse form and its codes.

c) When the reader attempts to become a writer, he takes on a social role.

Author and Narrator

The author can have a range of relationships with his narrator, from near total agreement to total disagreement. We must never presuppose that they are identical.

Monology and Dialogy

MONOLOGY derives from the Greek *monos* (one), and *logos* (order). In a monological novel, the author behind the narrator seeks to maintain a dominant or controlling voice or vision behind the conflict of values he creates, and ultimately this results in the elimination or supression of opposing views, with the affirmation of the dominant view. This produces:

a) a text as conscious text which affirms the author's single set of values through monological closure;

b) an unconscious text which consists of all the suppressed values or what is not said, the silences.

DIALOGY comes from the Greek *dia* (across) and here the writer allows several voices (polyphony) and visions (dialogy) to compete equally without bringing down closure and affirming a single set of values.

Narrator and Narrattee

a) The novelist does not talk to himself in any important sense, because his self has been socially reproduced like the self of others. He shares a sociolect or common set of social presuppositions with others.

b) Mediated through the narrator and the discourse form, the author speaks to a narrattee, who is inside the text, and remains there. We will sometimes find this made explicit when the narrator addresses the narrattee directly.

c) We become aware of the narrattee through the writer's use of social codes. These were quite familiar to the narrattee in the text, but the passage of time and change, or the fact that we may not share either the cultural milieu or the class of the narrattee of the text, may make them less familiar to us.

d) Were there such a thing as an ideal reader, we would hear the narrator speaking to us IMMEDIATELY in works from the past. In fact we hear MEDIATELY, which is to say that we do not so much hear with the narrattee as overhear what is being said to the narrattee.

Codes

Texts are constructed out of a series of codes, all of which can be called, in the broadest sense, cultural codes:

a) In the Hermeneutic Code, *hermeneus* (interpreter) comes from the Greek and *codex* from the Latin. The codes are to be decoded in the manner of spy work. The hermeneutic code is a product of the way in which discourse plays across the abstract chronological story so as to anticipate (PROLEPSIS) events, to withhold information (ANALEPSIS) with a view to creating reader suspense. The hermeneutic or interpretive code reveals these anticipations and retrospections.

b) The GENERIC CODE refers to the codes of the Literary genres in which the writer is working, always remembering that the writer is likely to be changing this code through his concrete practice.

c) The SYMBOLIC CODE takes account of the way symbols interconnect and work in a text to give focus and meaning to the text.

d) The CULTURAL CODE really is a plurality of codes ranging from dress, through food, sport, linguistic, social, economic, political, religious, and so on.

Author, Narrator, and Focalization

In his active social role as writer, the author brings his narrator into existence. This narrator will be of a certain kind in order to accomplish a certain philosophical function. We can define the narrator

a) in relation to his position in the story;

b) by the degree to which he remains in this position.

Narrator's Position and Story

The narrator as FOCALIZER, the one who provides the focus on persons and events, can occupy three main positions: a) external; b) internal; and c) internal and external.

External Focalizer

The EXTERNAL FOCALIZER is the third person narrator who seeks to hide behind his narration. He sees objects and events from the outside as an omnipresent (L. *omni*=all), omniscient (L. *scientia*=knowledge) viewer. A transcendental (beyond experience) narrator like a God, this narrator will sometimes enter his world, and this he does in basically two ways:

a) deliberately breaking objectivity by addressing the narrattee (Dickens does this to break the illusion of objectivity and to remind the reader that he is reading a text and not seeing the "real" world);

b) moving from direct discourse (as when a character is reported in the following manner: " 'This is nice,' he said") to free indirect discourse (as when the narrator enters the mind of the same character: "And it was so nice here"). The narrator here moves from transcendence to immanence (L. *in* = in; *manere* = to put; to put within things).

Internal Focalizer

The INTERNAL FOCALIZER or first person narrator is limited by the fact that he does not have a transcendental spot on which to stand and hear all and see all. He is therefore not parallel with God; though, immanent like Christ, he may have more than usual powers. Generally he is limited to what he sees, what he hears, and what he interprets. Like the transcendental narrator, he remains on the outside of minds even though he is among things, and like the transcendental narrator he may enter minds with free indirect discourse.

Internal and External Narrators

In this approach the writer attempts to have the advantages of both worlds, to be transcendentally above space and time while yet being within things. Typically such a text will oscillate between the two positions.

Examples of Discourse

a) DIRECT DISCOURSE: "Very good," he said.

b) INDIRECT DISCOURSE: Very good, he thought.

c) FREE INDIRECT DISCOURSE: He thought this was very good.

Metacritique

An analysis of the codes that constitute character, and of the conflict between characters and value codes in a text, as well as of the values affirmed in the closure of realist texts, will leave us with some sense of the world vision of the writer. This is most especially so if we do the same analysis with a number of a writer's texts and compare the similar, related or changing patterns. However, to get a fuller sense of the vision of a text, and where we and our own values stand in relation to a text, we need to go outside the text (take the brackets off the empirical world). We do this to determine what is absent from the apparently complete but closed off textual world as a whole. In this way we learn to see what the text does not say, as well as what it does say. By approaching texts in stages in this manner, we avoid the one-to-one naive realist equation between the characters of texts and characters of the empirical world.

Metacritique and Metanarrative

Were we to leave our analysis at the point where we have developed some understanding of the author's world vision, and a clear awareness of our individual and collective attitudes towards it, we would have gone a long way. However, we would not have begun to get at the deepest level of meaning in a literary text, a level of meaning behind all the competing meanings generated by Literary critics, meaning beyond Literature but perpetuated by it. To do this we must proceed through Literary-historical-philosophical analysis to a larger understanding that is well worth the not inconsiderable effort.

In order to begin this investigation, we can turn to Jean François Lyotard's conclusions in his *Report on Post-Modern Knowledge* (Lyotard, a Parisian professor, was commissioned by the Quebec universities to do this study). Our Euro-American culture, he tells us, has been sustained since The Enlightenment (17th-18th c.) by a number of metanarratives. These master narratives, or what we might want to call tribal myths (Gk. *mythos*=story), have informed and sustained our culture over time. These metanarratives, Lyotard insists, have broken down, and no longer command the belief of the people. The result is that we now live in the midst of a cultural crisis of major proportions.

The Metanarrative of Progress

One key metanarrative coming down to us from The Enlightenment is that of ''progress'', the idea that mankind (i.e. Euro-America) has been involved in a historical, stage-by-stage ascent from savagery to civilization, and is heading towards some TELOS (Gk. *telos*=goal) in which all problems will be resolved, all sorrows will cease, and sadness will end. This particular narrative has lost its power to command belief. For example, without denying all the spectacular technological achievements of post-Renaissance humanity, more and more people find themselves compelled to note that the level of misery in the world has not been significantly changed by all this progress, for what has been called progress has introduced new kinds of misery. Indeed, the nuclear bomb, an amazing piece of science and technology, could put an end to all human life. As Ruskin observed in the later nineteenth century, with the great ''wealth'' of industrialism has come also a great ''illth'', in the form of things that are bad for human beings.

Metanarrative and Dialectics

The metanarrative of progress sees a series of leaps over time, from one level of cultural stabilization to another, through a process of conflict and crisis of the kind we are now in. Expressed in graphic terms, progress would look like the arches of a bridge:

historical time

|———————|————————|————————|————————|————————|————————|

Each of these stages or arches represents a three-part process:

equilibrium——disequilibrium——equilibrium

This three-part movement from order through disorder to a new order recalls Hegel (1770-1831) and his dialectic:

thesis——antithesis——synthesis

Here a particular stabilization or order called the THESIS generates its opposite, the CONTRADICTION, which is the ANTI-THESIS, and enters into conflict with it. This struggle produces a SYNTHESIS or new stabilization, which contains elements of both thesis and antithesis, but at a higher level of development in the historical system. However, while the NEGATION of the thesis by the antithesis produces the synthesis on a new level of order, this synthesis never escapes from the broad framework of values which contain both thesis and antithesis (homeorhesis).

To escape from that broad framework, the act of negation which creates a synthesis would have to perform a second act of negation that would be the NEGATION OF THE NEGATION (the negation of the negation which is the synthesis). In this double action, the synthesis would in part negate the thesis and antithesis, but would in turn itself be immediately negated so as to get out of its own framework entirely and into a new framework of values (morphogenesis, see p. 63). We may view post-modernist Literature either as the antithesis of the thesis which is realism, or as a synthesis which remains defined by opposition to that realism which it sought to replace.

Metanarrative, Dialectic and Realist Text

The basic narrative structure of the realist text parallels the movement of the dialectic while also being a microcosmic version of the macrocosmic metanarrative of progress:

Realist Text:	equilibrium——disequilibrium——equilibrium
Dialectic:	thesis——antithesis——synthesis
Metanarrative:	sequences of the above in an ascending order.

This relationship means that behind the basic structure of the realist text (the offspring) lie the parents (the metanarrative of progress and the dialectic). Built into the very structure of the realist text, therefore, is the ideology of progress.

146

The Main Textual Code

Major and Minor Codes

Major codes are the social, psychological, economic, political, moral, inter-textual, and religious codes which may dominate a text. Each one of these codes contains in some degree the other codes, and two or more in combination, along with minor codes (food, dress etc.), are capable of dealing with the terrain of other major codes without openly doing so.

We can now see clearly that the main code of the realist text is not the generic code we tried out earlier, but the social code of the metanarrative of linear progress which determines the realist generic code itself. That is what determines the limits of what can be said.

Unified Ego, Closure, and Massaging

The realist text takes the reader through a vicarious dislocation of the ego. It deconstructs the ego of the reader by taking him through a conflict that results in a restabilization of the ego. The whole process thus affirms the existence of a unified ego. That is the whole concealed cultural-ideological purpose of the realist text, the most profound meaning of these texts. In a most tricky conjuring act, the realist text keeps the reader's consciousness concentrated on particular conflicts between characters over value. But behind these surface conflicts (which are so "real" for readers from the political left and the right as well), the "real" work of social reproduction goes on. Undisturbed, the realist text proceeds to restructure and reproduce, *behind the back of consciousness*, the sense of a unified "I". This ideological process explains the massaging effect of these realist readerly texts: they take a reader through a process of controlled disruption to affirm the unified ego, thus to make him feel that he "has", or "is", a "free" unified ego and individual. Yet, as the accelerating rate of mental illness in our culture tells us, as the crime rate, general disquiet and our own disturbed dreams remind us, the notion of a unified ego at the present time is a lie. We are rather a mosaic of loosely connected roles in a culture which is in a very serious state of crisis.

Metanarrative and Perception

With odd exceptions (Sterne's *Tristram Shandy* is a classic) our predecessors could not see the metanarrative of progress that lay behind the realist text. The reason why we can see the fundamental structures of the metanarrative of progress in the structures of its offspring, the realist text, is because the metanarrative itself has collapsed in ruins, bringing down the realist text with it. At least it has done so for all those who have eyes to see. Were that not so, we would be unable to see the structures that some of us now can see. "The owl of Minerva flies at dusk", Hegel said. By this he meant that wisdom (Minerva) comes late, and does so in the sense that we only become aware of the fundamental presuppositions of our thought when they have ceased to be fundamental presuppositions. To be able to see the presuppositions of realist thought so clearly tells us that we are already in another age.

Educated and Uneducated Readings

One common elitist view has it that the uneducated reader reads for mere entertainment, and usually reads intellectually and morally unedifying material as well, while the educated reader reads "Great Literature" from "The Canon" for a variety of morally and intellectually uplifting reasons. From the point of view of the metacritique which perceives the structuring of the realist text by the metanarrative of progress, this distinction is irrelevant. Both kinds of reader have been educated in the very same way behind their backs into the belief in a unified ego and a belief in progress.

How Real Was Realism?

If we keep our textual worlds of all kinds separate from the empirical worlds of all kinds across history, we must conclude that all we know for sure when we seek to explain in some way the empirical world by an explanatory textual world is our own explanation itself. How well the explanation fits its object we cannot know until events refute the explanation, in which case we must find ourselves another tentative explanation which will serve our purposes. We cannot have unmediated knowledge of the external world, as is well known in post-modern physics. We are all like the physicist Schrodinger looking at the closed box with the cat in it. To the question "Is the cat dead or alive there inside that box?" we can only answer for sure that if we say the cat is alive, then the cat is alive, and if we say that the cat is dead, then the cat is dead. We can only "know" our textual mediations of the thing, for that is the form the thing takes for us in our time.

Realism was "Real"

The physical world exists but reality is a social construction. Readers in past centuries were inscribed at the deep level of the presuppositions of thought itself with a belief in the metanarrative of progress, and in a corresponding belief in the existence of a unified ego. That social construction was THE reality of our ancestors, and therefore the realist text was a "real" reflection of reality for them. The basic linear pattern, the struggle and progress leading to closure in the realist novel matched perfectly the inner inscriptions by society, in individuals, of the metanarrative of progress. In this way, Literature quite literally replaced religion as a means of creating social cohesion. Realist texts, however, can no longer reflect the same reality because the realist construction no longer has credibility. Our everyday experience in fragmented, modern urban society disrupts our illusion of the unity of the ego and as well calls into question the metanarrative of progress. Out of these ruins emerges post-modern Literature.

PART II
APPLICATION OF ELEMENTS OF PROSE CRITICISM

Diegesis, Mimesis, Realism and Charles Dickens' *Hard Times*

"Now, what I want is Facts. Teach these boys and girls nothing but Facts. Facts alone are wanted in life. Plant nothing else, and root out everything else. You can only form the minds of reasoning animals upon Facts: nothing else will ever be of any service to them. This is the principle on which I bring up my own children, and this is the principle on which I bring up these children. Stick to the facts, Sir!"

The scene was a plain, bare, monotonous vault of a schoolroom, and the speaker's square forefinger emphasised his observations by underscoring every sentence with a line on the schoolmaster's sleeve. The emphasis was helped by the speaker's square wall of a forehead, which had his eyebrows for its base, while his eyes found commodious cellarage in two dark caves, overshadowed by the wall. The emphasis was helped by the speaker's mouth, which was wide, thin, and hard set. The emphasis was helped by the speaker's voice, which was inflexible, dry, and dictatorial. The emphasis was helped by the speaker's hair, which bristled on the skirts of his bald head, a plantation of firs to keep the wind from its shining surface....

So begins Dickens' novel, *Hard Times*.

As Raymond Williams remarks in *Keywords*:

151

Realism was a new word in the nineteenth century. It was used in French from the 1830's and in English from the 1850's. It developed four distinguishable meanings: 1) a term to describe, historically, the doctrines of Realists [i.e. universals are real] as opposed to those of nominalists [universals are merely names]; 2) a term to describe new doctrines of the physical world as independent of mind or spirit, in the sense sometimes interchangeable with naturalism or materialism; 3) as a description of facing up to things as they REALLY are, and not as we imagine or would like them to be...; 4) as a term to describe a method or an attitude in art or literature—at first an exceptional accuracy of representation, later a commitment to describing REAL events and showing things as they actually exist.

The second and third of these definitions about the physical world as objective and independent of mind, along with the fourth definition about art as a reflection of reality, reveal a common impulse from a changing society taking two parallel, independent, but mutually reinforcing directions, the one in realist or positivist science, the other in Literature.

In our day, these nineteenth-century scientific definitions have been smashed by avant-garde post-modernist physics, which allows that the physical world exists independently of mind, but insists that it can only be known through the filters of mind and the measuring instruments produced by mind, both of which influence all that they observe. In short, what we get when we look at empirical reality depends entirely upon the mind set, and the instruments of the mind set, which we take to it to do the looking. The fourth definition, having to do with art as a reflection of reality, has also come under attack: from the direction of post-modernist writing itself, and from post-modernist criticism. The result has been, as Williams puts it, that:

> REALIST art or literature is [now] seen as simply one convention among others, a set of representations, in a particular medium to which we have become accustomed. The object is not really lifelike but by convention and repetition has been made to appear so.

We might note here that while Williams is perfectly correct, the message has been very slow in getting around to English Departments.

If we return to the matter of the appearance of the new "realism" around 1850, we must note that hot on the heels of its emergence came Dickens' *Hard Times* in 1854. The first chapter of this text alone (the better part of which consists of the first two paragraphs quoted above) reveals Dickens involved, on the level of literature, in the ideological struggles of his hard times in the empirical world of Victorian society. It soon becomes clear that he was no friend of the new realism. Indeed, in this first chapter, he attacks realism on two fronts, as we shall see.

To begin to understand the achievement in *Hard Times*, we must recall the fundamental principle of the SIGN in semiotics: the sign is a binary system consisting of a material signifier which serves as the vehicle for the mental or signified concept. The sign refers to some object or process either outside in the empirical world, or inside thought and language itself. More often than not, as in *Hard Times*, we deal with sequences of signifieds fused through semiosis. The success of the Dickens passages above consists in this: Dickens not only gives expression to his vision through the channel of his signifieds on the semantic plane, but he does so through a perfectly appropriate use of the signifiers as well, revealing himself to be a masterful manipulator of signs on the plane of expression as well.

The opening short chapter of *Hard Times* clearly presents the unnamed speaker, Gradgrind, as the enemy. Dickens accomplishes this in two ways: through Gradgrind's own utterences in the first paragraph, and through the narrator's description in the second. These are, in fact, two different versions of the same thing, for Gradgrind does not really speak as an independent being, but is made to do so by the ''other'', the narratorial voice behind Gradgrind's voice, and behind this, the voice of Dickens.

We meet irony in Gradgrind's utterances. Gradgrind insistently demands that nothing but facts be taught to the children. ''Facts'' means facts according to realism in the positivist phase. ''Facts'' means the literal and unembellished truth in atomic units. ''Facts'' means atomic units of semantic meaning, Sir, without any recourse to theory. ''Facts'' means bits without reference to the totality of understanding. Yet facts trap Gradgrind. Or rather Gradgrind is made, ironically, to trap himself. He does not ''stick'' to the facts.

For the doctrinaire positivist mind, metaphors are not facts, but distortions of facts. Yet Gradgrind says we must ''plant'' facts, ''root out everything else'', and ''Stick to the facts''. We can, of course, plant potatoes, we can root out weeds, but we positively cannot do that with facts. Nor can we can ''stick'' to facts. Again, we have to see irony in this context. Gradgrind insists that he has only one set of principles and that he applies these equally to his own privileged children as well as to poor under-privileged children. We discover here that with the poor he is just a narrow-minded authoritarian bully, but with his own children, he becomes a fool as well.

The DESCRIPTION in the second paragraph demonstrates for us the full force of Dickens' technique and vision. The narrator, and Dickens behind him, oppose Gradgrind and Gradgrindism. This means that Dickens opposes the new realism in its positivist and other guises. Simply stated, he reveals on the level of the material signifying system, in his writing practice on the plane of expression, that an observer cannot discard his subjectivity and view objectively the external material world. This puts Dickens in the realm of literature where the great Heisenberg was to be in Physics some eighty years later. He makes his position clear through the development of his narrator, who becomes an important character in the novel.

In the realist novel, the literary equivalent of the objective observer of the now old positivist science is the omniscient, transcendent, third person narrator. He seeks to conceal himself, but silently claims to be giving us what appears to be an objective account of persons, places, processes and events. This silent presence characteristically does its work in such a way as to cause the reader to slide backwards and forwards between the textual world and the empirical world and thereby to utterly confuse the two. As a result, the typical reader of the typical realist novel feels that he/she has dealt with the real (i.e. empirical) world. Dickens takes this convention of silence, deliberately turns it inside out, and thus stresses his belief that there can be no transcendental or privileged viewing position from which anyone can view the world objectively. He sets up a third person narrator, to be sure, but refuses to hide or silence him. Going further, to stress the point, he undermines all pretensions to objectivity by foregrounding his material signifying system in the descriptive second paragraph. This he does through devices of repetition ("square", "emphasis", "facts", etc.). In this way he foregrounds both his medium and his narrator.

There is, however, more to this opening chapter and these first two paragraphs. Dickens sets up a debate here between Literary forms and Ideologies that goes back, in our culture, to Socrates, Plato and Aristotle. First, we must note that when we read, listen to, and see Gradgrind in this first paragraph, we could just as well be looking at the script of a play as reading a novel. It is a classic example of MIMESIS or a claimed "direct reflection" of "reality" in which the speaker apparently speaks for himself without any clear sign of narratorial intrusion. Of course, behind this voice hides the narrator, who sets up the ironies we find there. These ironies, in fact, arise out of a conflict between the narrator's (and Dickens') values and Gradgrind's. This mimesis SHOWS, rather than TELLS or TALKS or NARRATES about.

The second paragraph of description TELLS rather than SHOWS. It is thus diegesis or diegetic description rather than mimesis. Mimesis belongs to Aristotle, diegesis to his teacher, Plato, who objected to mimesis. He did so on the grounds that it can be a misleading or erroneous illusion of reality, rather than the "reality" (i.e. one-to-one reflection of the inner structure of empirical "reality") that it purports to be. Plato mistrusts mimesis because it hides the mediating narrator (and author) who must invariably insert some views or attitudes of their own. While mimetic realism purports to name, in an IMMEDIATE way, a so-called reality "out there" in the empirical world, it "really" MEDIATES recognizable elements of common experience and reconstitutes them in terms of the ideology of the creator. Thus, mimetic realism is always ideological. It constitutes its own object by causing us to see the world in its terms. In this way, illusion takes on the appearance of truth and the appearance of truth makes the representation appear "real". If we agree with the ideology in a particular realist text we shall find the text somehow "real", because our inner mental structures and the outer Literary structures in the text match one another.

We must note, in this conflict between Plato and Aristotle, and between diegesis and mimesis, one thing that often gets forgotten. In more than the obvious sense, Plato and Aristotle are very different philosophers. When Aristotle lectured on what has come down to us as his *Poetics*, he did so very much as a practising philosopher and professor, in each discipline of which he would seem to have been of the first rank. This meant, of course, that he approached the objects of his scrutiny from the outside. In contrast, Plato, a philosopher and professor of the first rank as well, was also a poet on the order of what the Romantics would later call genius. As Giorgi Lukacs has so convincingly shown in his paper "The Intellectual Physiognomy of Literary Character", Plato, in the *Socratic Dialogues*, creates superb "realist types" who embody in their utterances (like Gradgrind), in their textual being, in their textual world, the essential philosophical vision that moves them. Plato also creates these convincing realist types in order to set them up for defeat at the hands of Socrates' own informing vision. In short, Plato knew about manipulation (the term is really propaganda) from the inside of his own practice.

Dickens will settle for neither Aristotle nor Plato. He sets up the classic example of mimesis in the first paragraph and then undercuts it with the diegesis of the second. However, he does not destroy the claims to "truth value" of Aristotle's mimesis in the first paragraph in order to side with Plato's diegesis in the second. He foregrounds his material signifying system there in order to foreground his narrator, to undercut his narrator, in order to destroy any notion of privileged position, of any transcendental position. In this way Dickens undermines any illusion that he is going to dispense any final truths. This having been said, he does not renounce the right to speak openly on key questions of the day. Rather, through the many resources of overdetermined prose, Dickens tells us that we must be very careful about any "ism" that claims a monopoly on "the truth".

By doing what he does in *Hard Times*, Dickens reveals a commonality with post-modernism on key levels of post-modernist writing. He could do this, of course, because he was combating realism even before it had become established in its positivist form.

Post-modernism deals with realism at a time when, for now at least, its energies seem to be spent. Moreover, post-modernism confronts readers who have become habituated to realism, because they have been inscribed by this culture to believe that, that the textual world of "realism" equals exactly the "real" (the "order" of the empirical world we all inhabit). Realism and readers inscribed with the values of naive realism are thus out of touch with the empirical world in which we live, a dangerous situation in our own "hard times", and a sad fate for what was once a truly radical and subversive Literary practice.

Ernest Hemingway's
"Hills Like White Elephants"

"Hills Like White Elephants" is a realist text in the short story genre which runs to 159 lines. In that space we find a beginning, a middle, and an end, with a parallel equilibrium and disequilibrium sequence, followed by a sudden return to the apparent equilibrium with which the text started. While these structures of strife or value conflicts are linear, the story as chronological sequence is not, though we may reconstruct it along the following essentially unidirectional lines.

Story

We find in this work, as abstract chronological sequence, an unnamed "the American", and "the girl", nicknamed "Jig", who have been travelling for an unstated extended period around Europe, staying in small hotels, and living out of suitcases. The two are lovers and the girl has become pregnant, an event which leads to some tension between them before this text starts, but which we do not discover on the level of the signifieds until some way into the text (though the material signifiers work even in the early stages to tell us that something has happened). Without any open signs of their differences, the two wait at a little railway station across the valley of the Ebro river in Spain. On a hot day, the pair sit outside in the shade and drink beer, changing drinks for a while, then shifting back to beer. They engage in apparently

157

desultory conversation, which leads to the suggestion by him that she do "it", the repeated "it" being the abortion which he refuses to name. She finally agrees to his constantly repeated suggestion after also listening to his reiteration that she make up her own mind about "it". The Madrid train arrives and they prepare to leave.

Discourse

As in many Hemingway short stories, interest is generated through PROLEPSIS, or the anticipation of future events. We find prolepsis in the first paragraph where the proleptic, the mention of the Madrid express, anticipates the end of the tale. The reverse technique, ANALEPSIS, provides information that has been withheld from us deliberately. This device we discover in the revelation that the girl is pregnant, a fact withheld from us until almost a third of the way through. The tension between prolepsis and analepsis creates the suspense we have been culturally inscribed to expect from this kind of realist discourse.

The Materialization of Space

In the opening paragraph, Hemingway deliberately piles DETERMINERS (so called because they cause us to anticipate nouns that follow) of the definite article variety, on top of one another. He does this to establish the materiality of his space. Thus we proceed through the anaphorically linked and mutually supportive eight-line opening sequence of "the hills", "the valley", "the...shadow", "the building", "the...door", "the bar", "The American", "the girl", "the shade", "the building", "the express". One of the linguistic means for aiding in this sense of materiality of the definite articles is the practice of opposing to them some indefinite article determiners which then change into definite article determiners, the move from the indefinite to the definite suggesting an increasing solidity and definiteness of things. In the opening lines we find "a curtain" and "a table", which get transformed within a few lines into "the curtain" and "the table". In the immediately following lines the serving woman appears in the text as "a woman" (in line 14) to become "the woman" on line 16. These transformations add to the growing sense of concreteness, a transforming illusion of the signifieds which gives us the impression of the "real". The fact of not giving "the" man and "the" girl proper names also has the effect of giving them a material emphasis because of their place in the anaphoric chain of determiners. This linking we shall find to be central to the theme, for the text in these early lines already works at thematizing the problematic.

Deixis

The determiners in the first paragraph serve the function of deictics which locate the man and woman in the sense of giving them existence in place. They also locate them, and the narrator, in relation to space and time. The deictic "across" in "across the valley" of the first line locates the narrator and the pair through a here/there situation. So does the deictic "this" in "on this side", and "between", in "the station was between two lines of rails". Hemingway's deictic "against" in "Close against the side of the station" locates in turn a shadow, curtain, door, and bar. Then the deictics "at", "in", and "outside" specify location. The deictics of "Madrid", "Barcelona", and "express" obviously locate the station in space but also introduce, for the first time, the dectics of time with the future tense "would come", and with "forty minutes" ("the express from Barcelona would come in forty minutes. It stopped at this junction for two minutes and went on to Madrid"). In the latter sentence "this" is a deictic of space (also locating the narrator), while "stopped for two minutes" is a deictic of time, as is "and went on".

Narration

The narrator is a third person omniscient narrator who does not speak of events in the past, because the action clearly goes on in front of him. Yet he uses past tense verbs. Why? This is a convention which has nothing necessarily to do with pastness, and everything to do with the need for the narrator to distance himself from his narration, his need to appear transparent so that we do not see him. The past tense verb is therefore a pseudo past tense verb (see pp. 180-81).

Having and Being

The text revolves around the problematic of having and being, a central problem in our culture of consumerism. Rootless consumer culture, embodied in the vulgar materialist "The American", considers the "having" or possession or acquisition of material things and experiences as the *summum bonum* (L., the highest good) of all existence, while "being" consists solely of "being rooted in" (materialist) places. The former is after goods or products, the latter after "the good". We see this dualism emerge in the two different meanings of "having" in a key passage (the lines below are marked "m" for man, "w" for woman):

159

"And we could have all this [the place]," she said. "And we could have everything and every day we make it more impossible."

"What did you say?" [m]

"I said we could have everything." [w]

"We can have everything." [m]

"No, we can't." [w]

"We can have the whole world." [m]

"No, we can't." [w]

"We can go everywhere." [m]

"No, we can't. It isn't ours any more." [w]

"It's ours." [m]

"No, it isn't. And once they take it away, you never get it back." [w]

"But they haven't taken it away." [m]

"We'll wait and see." [w]

His acquisitive notion of the whole earth as property that can be dominated, can be had, contrasts with her anguished sense of absence, of not being possessed, had, by the material earth to which she feels she belongs.

I and Thou

The positions of the man and girl correspond to Martin Buber's concept of I-it and I-thou relationships. The American represents the instrumental I of domination, which seeks to control the other and subordinate her, and the whole earth, to his wishes. He succeeds in subordinating her. She does not wish to dominate the earth as if it were property, but seeks rather an I-thou relationship of caring with the man. She fails, and changes to his way of thinking.

Hills and Elephants

The two views about "having" find a reflection in the lines out of which the title comes:

"They [the hills] look like white elephants," she said.
"I've never seen one," the man drank his beer.
"No, you wouldn't have."

The two kinds of having appear here in the form of two kinds of seeing. His is the cold, factual, positivist mind (give me the facts), hers the intuitive metaphorical mind of the imagination. She sees with open-ended logic that can suggest the living nature of nature; he can only see cold material exteriors, property. There is more to the white elephant, as we shall see.

Shifters

The determiners in the first paragraph serve the function of deictics which locate the man and woman in the sense of giving them existence in place. They also locate them, and the narrator, in space and time. The deictic "across" in "across the valley" of the first line locates the narrator and the pair through a here/there situation. So does the deictic "this" in "on this side", and "between", in "the station was between two lines of rails". Hemingway's deictic "against" in "Close against the side of the station" locates in turn a shadow, curtain, door, and bar.

In this text we have "the American", who has not been given a proper name, and "the girl" with the nickname "Jig", who has no proper name either. Through this absence of proper names, the text tells us to look at the possibility that these characters are types representing forces larger than the individual. Simultaneously it compels us to look carefully at the pronouns.

Pronouns and Users

The personal pronouns used by the narrator, "the American", and "the girl" follow:

Narrator of the American:
   a)   the American
   b)   the man
   c)   he

Narrator of the girl:
   a)   the girl
   b)   she

American of self:
   a)   I

American of girl:
   a)   Jig
   b)   you
   c)   it (the foetus)

Girl of self:
   a) I
   b) it (the foetus)

Of each other:
   a) we
   b) us
   c) it (the foetus)

Of others:
   a) they (with several significations)

The Shifting "I"

In this text the instrumental "I" of the American does not change. It manipulates the girl until her "I" changes to become like his by falling into orbit around his value system. We see this clearly at the end of the text:

> "Doesn't it [the foetus] mean anything to you? We could get along" [she said].
> "Of course it does. But I don't want anybody but you. I don't want any one else. And I know it's [the abortion] perfectly simple."
> "Yes, you know it's perfectly simple."
> "It's all right for you to say that, but I do know it [is perfectly safe]."

These lines lead the way to the concluding two lines which reveal that she has shifted:

> "Do you feel better?" he asked.
> "I feel fine," she said. "There's nothing wrong with me. I feel fine."

White Elephants and Hills

Hemingway's title makes an obvious intertextual allusion to the story of the white elephant: An Indian Prince once found himself in possession of a white elephant which, unlike other elephants, was eating him out of palace and peace of mind. To resolve his problem he gave it as a gift to a neighbouring prince whom he did not like. The title implies that the girl cannot spiritually afford the gift the American gives her—himself.

Thematizing the Problematic

The text starts working early on the continuing anaphoric repetition of the neuter pronoun "it". In this context "it" proves to be a shifter with truly chameleon-like qualities. We find two consecutive sentences beginning with "it" at the end of the first paragraph:

> "It was very hot and the express for Barcelona would come in forty minutes. It stopped at this junction for two minutes and went on to Madrid."

The first "it" here is ambiguous, fuzzy, and could mean any or all of hot day, hot weather, hot afternoon, hot climate. The second "it" has precision, for it refers directly to the express. These two uses of "it" parallel the two senses of I and the two senses of the hills, the "I" as an "it", looking at hills as "it", as opposed to the "I" as a "thou" looking at others as "thou" and nature as "living being".

Hemingway makes sure that we do not miss this "it" dualism when he repeats the pattern in the two sentences which follow the above:

> "What should we drink?" the girl asked. She had taken off her hat and put it on the table.
> "It's pretty hot," the man said.

The second "it" has the same fuzzy reference as we saw above, while the first one has precision, referring to "hat". For a succession of thirty lines we then get a number of cumulative references to "it":

> "They've painted something on it [the beaded curtain]," she said.
> "What does it [the painting] say?" [woman]
> "Anis Del Toro. It's a drink." [man]
> "Could we try it?" [w]
> "Is it good with water?" [w]
> "It's all right." [m]
> "It tastes like licorice." [w]
> [They proceed to argue.]
> "Oh, cut it [decidedly ambiguous pronoun reference] out." [m]
> "You started it [argument]." [w]
> "That's all we do, isn't it [some vagueness]—look at things and try new drinks?" [w]
> "It's [beer is] lovely," the girl said.

Through this heavy emphasis on "it", the text forces us to focus on "it" as a sign or key word. The "it" sequence, in fact, prepares the vulgar materialist way to the double signified "it", the man's Freudian slip: "Oh, cut it out." Here the immediate reference through cliché is to her argument. On another level, however, the man reveals his impatience with the failure of the girl to conform to his manipulations through his protestations that she can make up her own mind about the abortion. His slip gives the lie to all that. In Rifaterre's terms, the "oh, cut it out" Freudian slip is the cliché which generated the text.

Verb, Tense, Aspect, and Narration

"Hills Like White Elephants" begins:

> The hills across the valley of the Ebro were long and white. On this side there was no shade and no trees and the station was between two lines of rails in the sun. Close against the side of the station there was the warm shadow of the building and a curtain, made of strings of bamboo beads, hung across the open door into the bar, to keep out flies. The American and the girl with him sat at a table in the shade, outside the building. It was very hot and the express from Barcelona would come in forty minutes. It stopped at this junction for two minutes and went on to Madrid.
> "What should we drink?" the girl asked. She had taken off her hat and put it on the table.
> "It's pretty hot," the man said.

Despite the past tense verbs in these lines from Hemingway's realist short story, we have a clear sense that this scene and action happen in front of us. This is because these verbs are not, despite appearances, past tense verbs, but pseudo past tense verbs. They do not function to set an action in the past, but rather to distance the narrator (to remove himself either spatially and/or temporally) from his narration in the traditional manner of third person omniscient narrators. In this way the narrator seeks to conceal himself from the eyes of those who believe in the "reality", the unconstructed condition, of realist texts.

If the third person narrator can conceal something in the interests of the narration, the verb tense itself can hide things from unknowing eyes. In particular, it can keep ASPECT out of the field of vision of the believing reader. This is a complex subject in general, but with specific reference to narration we can isolate aspectual usages of the progressive verb tense. That tense reveals an ongoing process as opposed to an event located in time within the ongoing process. As John Lyons observes in his two-volume *Semantics*: "the English progressive [tense] may be used in the historical mode as a state or process within which some other situation, represented as an event, is temporally located.'' He cites as a trivial example ''John was reading when Mary came in'', and notes that ''Mary's entry is represented as an event occurring as an event at some point within the period during which John's reading was going on.''

Literary usages of the progressive verb tense are abundant. Carson McCullers starts her story ''A Tree, A Rock, A Cloud'' as follows:

> It was raining that morning, and still very dark. When the boy reached the streetcar cafe he had almost finished his route and he went in for a cup of coffee. The place was an all-night cafe owned by a bitter and stingy man called Leo.

The past progressive ''was raining'' sets up the ongoing (umbrella) cover of process which distances the narrator from her narration, while allowing the actions of ''reached'', ''had...finished'', ''went'', and so on, to occur within the progressive verb tense process.

We find the same thing in Flannery O'Connor's ''Judgement Day'':

> Tanner was conserving all his strength for the trip home. He meant to walk as far as he could get and trust to the Almighty to get him the rest of the way. That morning and the morning before, he had allowed his daughter to drive him and had conserved that much more energy.

The past progressive ''was conserving'' becomes the active containing process for the events that follow.

Irony

There is another meaning of ''white elephant'' which makes the title of this story a critique of the universal materialization of space and character the text creates. The obvious pun on ''white elephant'' in its garage-sale, church basement bazaar context, implies the reduction of the empirical world in the text to a status where everything (and everyone) in it has no value or purpose or use in and for itself. It implies that the materialism portrayed by the text is of the vulgar variety. The only ''value'' of ''white elephants'' in this context is the act of their acquisition. Thereafter, they are merely looked at, from a distance, but not used, handled, or, ultimately, enjoyed. They are at best curiosities, at worst useless objects, and ultimately their possession, considered important in the act of acquisition, becomes embarrassingly gauche. By allowing ''the American'' to persuade his companion (''the girl'') to ''see things his way'', by turning her, like everything around him, including the landscape, into a "white elephant", of interest to him only on the question as to whether or not he possesses it (her) as a material object, he has stopped the world (generation, procreation) and guaranteed that "the girl" will never be a lover—merely another bauble he possesses, a "white elephant". This reading is reinforced by the way in which the text "names" the female character, which in both instances is with a diminutive: with "the girl" (as opposed to "the woman"), and with a "nickname" (rather than a "proper" name). This, of course, must be seen in contrast to the way in which the text "names" the male character with "the American", which makes him much larger than naming him with a "proper name" ever could. This "naming" makes America "a man's world", and the male character of this story the embodiment of that ideology (that nation) itself. This text constitutes that ideology as "male chauvinist" in the truest sense of the word: an ideology which requires the transformation of all of the empirical world, including other persons, but especially women and children, into material objects, to be acquired and possessed by "man".

Edgar Allan Poe's
"The Fall of the House of Usher"

Edgar Allan Poe begins his "The Fall of the House of Usher" by simultaneously materializing and dematerializing the world so that all that is solid seems to melt into air:

> During the whole of a dull, dark and soulless day in the autumn of the year, when the clouds hung oppressively low in the heavens, I had been passing alone, on horseback, through a singularly dreary tract of country; and at length I found myself, as the shades of evening drew on, within view of the melancholy House of Usher. I do not know how it was—but, with the first glimpse of the building, a sense of insufferable gloom pervaded my spirit. I say insufferable; for the feeling was unrelieved by any of the half pleasurable, because poetic, sentiment, with which the mind usually receives the sternest natural images of the desolate and the terrible.

Poe materializes and dematerializes his world here through two strings of determiners, the indefinite article "a" and the definite article "the":

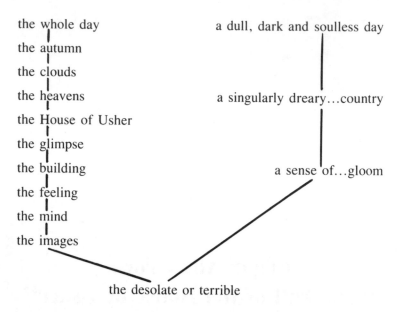

the whole day

the autumn

the clouds

the heavens

the House of Usher

the glimpse

the building

the feeling

the mind

the images

a dull, dark and soulless day

a singularly dreary...country

a sense of...gloom

the desolate or terrible

Here we see a dialectical process. The solidity of the discernible noun objects represented by most of the definite articles plays off against the indefinite and undermining feelings attached to the indefinite pronouns. Meanwhile, the definiteness of the definite articles moves inwards from the outside "things" into the mind with "the feeling...the mind...the images". Both strings of articles find their target in the very abstract, mysterious and unclear adjectives without nouns: "the desolate or terrible".

As Rosemary Jackson points out in *Fantasy*:

> "The Fall of the House of Usher" (1839) is Poe's most famous fantasy. Its narrative method exemplifies the process of "making strange" which characterizes the uncanny. The tale is introduced through a reflexive frame: a pool of water. Its narrator approaches then withdraws from the desolate house of Usher, as a place of death, with its "bleak walls, vacant eye-like windows, few rank sedges". The house is not given directly, but as a reflection, i.e. an inverted form itself....

As with fantasy in general, the function of Poe's text is to give witness to the dark underside of realism, to the things repressed by realism, to commit a transgression of taboos, in this instance that of incest. This is the relationship between Madeleine and Usher. As Jackson puts it, the characters do not exist as independent characters. They are generated by the narrator, produced through his trance-like condition as he stares into a dirty mirror image...on the edge of reality. The house and its inhabitants are "real" only to the narrator. He re-presents himself as the "other" through Usher, who enacts his fantasy life.

Sinclair Ross' "The Lamp at Noon"

Sinclair Ross' "The Lamp At Noon" is a classic realist text in the short story genre. It has a beginning, a middle, and an end, and starts ever so briefly with equilibrium, moving halfway through the first sentence into a hint of disequilibrium, and concludes with an end that both restores equilibrium and purports to have resolved the problematic. This end conceals a skilfully contrived closure. With the conclusion comes proof that this is a monological text in its affirmation of a single set of values. However, that resolution produces some problems because of an unresolved conflict between the socio-economic and religious codes, as we shall see.

LITERARINESS can be simply defined as the qualities of a literary sign sequence that announces a text as literature rather than the discourse of formal prose non-fiction, as in newspaper editorials (though note the comments on *TIME* earlier, p. 8). We can find abundant evidence of this in the first sentence of "The Lamp At Noon":

$$\breve{\text{A}}\ \acute{\text{litt}} \ // \ \breve{\text{le}}\ \breve{\text{be}} \ // \ \acute{\text{fore}}\ \acute{\text{noon}} \ // \ \text{sh}\breve{\text{e}}\ \acute{\text{lit}} \ // \ \text{th}\breve{\text{e}}\ \acute{\text{lamp}}.$$

We discover here a ten-syllable poetic line with a basic iambic pentameter rhythm. The pyrrhic second foot backgrounds itself in relation to the heavy or loud beat of the opening iambic foot, even as it allows a greater foregrounding of the spondaic third foot. This produces a creative ambiguity that allows us on the semantic level to read "before noon", but at the same time feel the semantically different "fore noon" because of the rhythmic manipulations.

That the iambic rhythm is no accident, we can learn from the first part of the second sentence, which confirms the iambic pattern:

$$\breve{\;}\;/\quad\breve{\;}\;/\quad\;/\;\;/\quad\breve{\;}\;/\quad\breve{\;}\;/$$
Dement // ed wind // fled keen // ing past // the house.

We can find further evidence of literariness in the signifying system of the first sentence. The alliteration of "little", "lit" (near rhyme), and "lamp" draws attention to the literary medium, something the discourse of formal prose non-fiction has traditionally avoided. The personification "Demented wind" works to the same end, attributing the human quality of madness to physical forces of nature. This personification is deepened by the metaphor "keening", an Irish peasant lament for the dead, to turn the wind into an Irish peasant mourner.

Viewed in relation to the semantic content of the first sentence, and to the thematic content of the whole text (microcosm to macrocosm), the syntax of the first sentence works through its semantics to cause that sentence to be the microcosmic part that states the problematic of the macrocosmic whole. Were the first sentence to be composed in linear form it would read:

She lit the lamp a little before noon.

This foregrounds the "She", visually through the upper case "S", and conceptually because this syntactical form makes her dominate events as the actor lighting the lamp. But the woman in the story does not dominate events, for the whole problematic reveals that she is dominated by mad nature and a patriarchal husband. That is why the dislocated sentence works so well:

A little before noon she lit the lamp.

Here the "she" gets backgrounded within the time and action to suggest her domination by events. Domination by events leads to disorder conveyed through the syntactical fragments of the second sentence:

Demented wind fled keening past the house: a wail through the eaves that died every minute or two.

The determiner "the" has been dropped from the first sign sequence.

Adding to the opening literariness, Ross repeats part of "A little before noon she lit the lamp" in the opening sentence of the second paragraph: "She lit the lamp". This linear sentence foregrounds the "she" as dominant actor to introduce the active side of the passive sufferer of the first paragraph, which will engage in the conflict the text composes.

171

Story

Ellen is the daughter of an urban shopkeeper who marries Paul, a young farmer
on the Canadian prairies. The fifth year of their marriage has brought a baby,
drought, dust storms, economic depression, poverty, and domestic disharmony.
The story begins in this fifth year with Ellen cooking and looking out on the
dust storm as she awaits the return of her husband. The pair have obviously
been fighting, and so she anxiously awaits his return. He returns, they fight
again, and he leaves to go and work in the barn. Ellen wants Paul to quit
farming and go and work for her father in his store. Paul wants the independent
existence of farming, and he clearly resents the fact that Ellen had correctly
warned him about his misuse of the land, his overworking of it such that the
wind is now blowing away all the topsoil. When Paul finally comes back
to the house, he finds the door open, the house empty. He calls on neighbours
to search for Ellen and the baby, but finally finds her himself. She has been
hiding from the wind behind a dune. The baby has died either from exposure
or from being held too close. With few words, and much said through gesture,
they become reconciled.

Closure

"The Lamp At Noon" concludes with the dust storm beginning to drop and
with the emergence of a red sky at night ("Red sky in the morning, sailor
take warning; red sky at night, sailor's delight"), the two characters having
reconciled their differences and come to a new understanding of each other.
Ross has them standing and looking out at this optimistic scene as he brings
his text to a thematic conclusion on the level of the signified. However, he
brings about closure on the level of the signifier as well as on the level of
the signified. He does this by returning to the iambic rhythms and manipulation
of syntax for semantic purposes of his first paragraph.

Discourse

Discourse plays across the story to produce what we call the hermeneutic
code. As noted, the work actually begins five years after the marriage and
we learn about this past as Ross analeptically reveals, piece by piece, that
which has been withheld from us through the dislocation of linear chronological
and causal sequences, even as he proleptically anticipates events, all with a
view to creating and maintaining reader interest.

The key proleptic or anticipatory device in "The Lamp at Noon" is
anaphora. There are a number of local instances of it, such as the repetition
of "window" at the beginning. The main structural one, however, is that

of names. We meet the "she" in the first line and many repetitions of it, but it is not until line 111 that we discover her name to be Ellen. Anaphora has been used to keep this information from us through the string of "she" pronouns. The introduction of the name Ellen works cataphorically or retrospectively to resignify all of the uses of "she" that preceded it.

Deixis

Deixis refers to the use of locative devices in order to establish persons, times and places in a text. The "she" and its repetitions establish the young woman, while "before noon" is a deictic of time. Through the use of deictics, the first few paragraphs establish relationships between house and barn and dust storm, sufficiently for us to know that the setting is the "dirty thirties".

Sex Role Code

Ross' text puts two sex role codes in conflict to create the problematic: that of Patriarchy in the form of Paul, who wishes to maintain a male dominance over a subordinated female, and that of a democratic Ellen, who wishes to have a relationship of equality with her husband.

Name Codes

"The Lamp at Noon" puts Greece at odds with Jerusalem through the name codes. The name Ellen means "the light" in Greek, and Paul's character obviously connects him with the misogynist St. Paul of the New Testament.

The Double-Double-Bind

Paul and Ellen are both constituted in a double-bind situation. Paul loves Ellen, but he also loves his patriarchal code. If he persists in maintaining his patriarchal values, he will lose Ellen. If he continues to love Ellen, but on her terms, in the democratic code, he must lose his patriarchal code. For her part, Ellen loves Paul, but also loves the democratic values she inherited from her petty bourgeois father. If she keeps her democratic values, she must leave, and lose, Paul. If she keeps Paul on his terms, she must lose her democratic values and self-respect.

The text resolves this impossible situation with some fast sleight-of-hand at the very end where Paul undergoes a swift and unmentioned conversion to Ellen's value system.

Ross' Ideology

As in so many of his other works, Ross asserts the values of democratic relations in the family and, by extension, in the larger society. We see in "The Lamp At Noon", however, that he does not demonstrate the superiority of democracy over patriarchy, so much as assert it.

The Religious Code

That the dust storm lasts three days, and that the baby dies on the third day to save the marriage and bring peace to the world, all suggest the religious code of Christianity.

The Economic Code

Behind the drought and dust storms of Ross' text lies the economic crisis of the Great Depression. That depression caused the foreclosure of many small farms, and anticipated the foreclosure of many others, from that day to this, as the costs of machinery and so on required fewer and bigger farms. Paul is caught in this crisis.

Conflict of Religious and Economic Codes

On the level of the religious code, the death of the baby works symbolically to suggest salvation for Paul and Ellen—a secular salvation, of course. On another level, however, the child serves as a symbol of future generations, and since this child dies, it serves to symbolize the absence of a future, a vision at odds with the religious code. Moreover, this vision also falls into conflict with the optimistic conclusion of Ross' text, where the symbolic red sky speaks of better days to come. It is as if Ross affirmed in his conclusion his optimistic vision on a conscious, level, but simultaneously undermined it on an unconscious level.

James Thurber's
"The Secret Life of Walter Mitty"

Story

The abstract chronological sequence which is the story begins with Walter Mitty driving towards Waterbury with his wife as his passenger. He drops her off at the hairdresser's shop, and she tells him that at his (middle) age he ought to be wearing gloves and ought to buy some overshoes in order to save his health. Mitty goes to his regular parking lot where the attendant soon tells him that he is in the wrong lane. Mitty hands him the keys and proceeds on foot in the direction of Main Street. There he buys overshoes and walks on, wondering what else his wife had told him to purchase. Finally, he remembers and, to the delight of passers-by, he blurts out "puppy biscuits". He proceeds to an A&P store where he buys the biscuits. The purchase made, he goes to the rendezvous point at the hotel to meet his wife, but discovers he is early. Picking up an old *Liberty* magazine, he sinks into a chair and emerges into consciousness again only at the sound of his wife scolding him for being difficult to find. They leave the hotel together. She remembers that she needs something from the drug store, so she tells Mitty to wait for her. He lights a cigarette, smokes it, flips away the butt, and continues to wait.

Discourse

The discourse of the short story genre plays across the abstract chronological sequence to dislocate the conventional linear flow, which generates reader interest by anticipation (prolepsis) and the retrospective release of withheld information (analepsis). Only through the analeptic "puppy biscuits" do we learn that Mitty had been told by his wife to get something else. That information had been withheld from us so, along with Mitty, we wonder why we cannot remember what it was. The title is a proleptic, for it offers us advance information.

Generic Codes

"The Secret Life of Walter Mitty" has two generic codes which are deliberately placed in conflict with one another. As the account of the story above would suggest, the text is informed by a "realist" code in the short story genre. Thurber opposes that with the fantasy code of the short story genre.

Fantasy and Subversion

Rosemary Jackson correctly subtitles her book *Fantasy as The Literature of Subversion*. She speaks of fantasy and the fantastic in the following way:

> "The fantastic exists as the inside, or underside, of realism, opposing the novel's closed monological forms with open dialogical structures, as if the novel had given rise to its own opposite, its unrecognizable reflection. Hence their symbiotic relationship....The fantastic gives utterance precisely to those elements which are known only through their absence within the dominant "realistic" order.

This describes exactly what happens in Thurber's text, for Thurber introduces his fantasy text, the "unconscious" of realist literature, into the same textual frame as the realist text in order to disrupt the latter.

Illusion and Reality

"Reality" here means the textual world of the realist text, and "illusion" here means the state of affairs in which that which *appears* to be "real", in the sense defined above; turns out not to be so. The text begins in the following way:

176

"We're going through!" The Commander's voice was like thin ice breaking.

This *appears* to be the beginning of a realist text, for we seem to have an *in medias res* beginning and an equilibrium that is about to give way to disequilibrium. In fact, the "realist" beginning turns out to be illusion. We discover Mitty to be in a dream world when the realist voice of his wife snaps him out of it:

"Not so fast! You're driving too fast!" said Mrs. Mitty. "What are you driving so fast for?"

Realism and Banality

The values emerging from the world of textual realism in "The Secret Life of Walter Mitty" reveal a banal, petty bourgeois existence of cars, of driving to stores, and of shopping (the key cultural activity in our society), along with a key concern over health in the interests of longevity and the continuance of that same banal social existence, in the interest of accumulating "quantity" rather than experiencing "quality".

Fantasy, the Grand Heroic and Double Disruption

The Grand Heroic fantasy world is made to subvert the banality of "real" petty bourgeois existence as it is represented in this textual world. But in a simultaneous movement the Grand Heroic is made to subvert itself. This is done through a pastiche treatment in which jarring fragments of different heroes are pasted together amidst mock collections of pseudo facts and fantasies (the hydroplane in the opening sequence is a ludicrous technical impossibility). The heroes are bits and pieces of the "Great" on Land, Sea, and in the Air from the past down to the World War II present at the time of writing.

Intertextuality Across Media

The "Great" heroes are not parodied directly from history, of course. On reading this text, we get a sense of *déjà vu* in the fantasy sections. And so *indeed* we have met them before: in Hollywood movies which treated these subjects seriously and set up the "Great" as role models. On this level, Thurber parodies the Hollywood treatments of "Heroes" to reduce them to size.

The Double

Thurber creates a classic "double" in his text. As Rosemary Jackson puts it in *Fantasy*:

> Fantastic character deformation suggests a radical refusal of the structures, the "syntax" of cultural order. Incoherent, fluid selves exist in opposition to precious portraits of individuals as whole or essential.

This catches Mitty perfectly, for the Mitty of the realist text is the bourgeois individual who is commonly taken to be "whole or essential", while the Mitty of the fantasy dream world is one of the "Incoherent, fluid selves [who] exist in opposition...."

Decentring the "I"

Thurber's text is witness to, and a literary example of, as Rosemary Jackson says, the process of "a gradual erosion of ideas of psychic unity over the past two centuries. Long before Freud, monistic definitions of the self were being supplanted by hypotheses of dipsychism (dual selves) and polypsychism (multiple selves)". This whole process has been part of the process of the deconstruction and decentring of the bourgeois notion of the individual, of removing the privileged position given to that individual by Renaissance society. Post-modern science has already ejected the individual from his privileged position as a supposedly neutral and objective observer of an objective Nature. It sees the individual as a participant *in* the nature he or she is involved in the process of viewing, not neutrally absent from it.

The result of the combined disruption of realism and fantasy is a Menippean satire (pp. 208-9) which profanes the sacred heroes of Hollywood (and the day), and refuses to affirm any values at all, other than a certain stoic notion of endurance.

Closure

Closure comes about, or is made to come about, with a return to the fantasy world with which the text began, but although this closure operates well to suggest that the text works and does not simply stop or end, it does not close off the ideological questions that it has raised, but leaves the text open-ended. Whereas realism concludes with monological closure, bringing to the surface the values that had dominated throughout, this text has no monological values to bring to the surface, for it is a dialogical text.

Stephen Leacock's
"The Conjurer's Revenge"

Story

A conjurer (we would now say magician) gives a public performance. A man in the front row disrupts this performance through his undermining comments. The conjurer has his revenge by smashing the man's watch, ruining his collar and hat and so on, while the man still believes this to be part of the illusion, which is the art of conjuring.

Discourse

The text begins *in medias res*; has a beginning, a middle, and an end; and it proceeds through the sequence of equilibrium, disequilibrium, equilibrium. Discourse plays across the story line (the abstract chronological sequence) to dislocate certain elements so as to create reader interest. The title works proleptically to anticipate the conclusion, and the past perfect tense verb "having shown" looks backward analeptically to give us the retrospective information that the conjurer has already shown his cloth to be empty.

Deixis

Deixis refers to the locative devices of language in a text. This text quickly establishes the essentials of time, place, and person:

> "Now, ladies and gentlemen," said the conjurer, "having shown you that the cloth is absolutely empty, I will proceed to take from it a bowl of goldfish. Presto!"
> All around the hall people were saying, "Oh, how wonderful."
> "How does he do it?"
> But the Quick Man on the front seat said in a big whisper to the people near him, "He—had—it—up—his—sleeve."

Deictics of Time

The deictics of time in these opening lines locate the time relations of this text. These include the adverb "Now", which gives the setting as the present time, the past perfect tense verb "having shown", which speaks of a completed action before the text opened, and the future tense verb "will", which refers here to the near future, the whole verb sequence linking past, present and future to locate precisely the temporal setting of the text. The historical time context of this time sequence remains unspecified, so the text appears to float freely in historical time.

Deictics of Space

These locate the spatial setting and spatial relationships of the text. They include "all around the hall", "front seat", and "near him", all seen in relation to the position of the conjurer and, as we shall see below, the narrator.

Deictics of Person

These locate persons in the text and they include here "the conjurer (I)", the "ladies and gentlemen" who are also "the people", the "you", "the Quick Man".

Narrator

The past tense verb "said" in the opening line indicates the presence of an omniscient, omnipresent third person narrator. We have a sense of immediacy created by this opening scene that makes it seem to be going on in front of us, while the past tense verb would suggest that it is not. This contradiction reveals the verb to be a pseudo past tense verb. Rather than an actual reference to the past, this verb serves to distance the narrator from his narration. It is a means whereby the narrator will be made to disappear from a realist text for those who are habituated to realist texts.

Framing Verbs

The past tense verb "having shown" leads into the progressive tense "were saying" to act as the verbal frame of process within which *particular* acts and events represented by other verbs operate (see above).

Proxemics

PROXEMICS refers to the spatial relationships between persons and persons, and persons and things. In this text there is a non-proximal relationship of space between the narrator and the time framing process along with its contained acts and events. We see also a hierarchy of relationships involving the Quick Man and the audience; and the conjurer, the Quick Man, and the audience. Putting the Quick Man in the front row close to the conjurer causes the relations of spatial proximity to represent the hierarchy of importance of these two characters in the text.

Character and Intertextuality

In the manner of most realist characters, the conjurer and the Quick Man have a certain convincing illusion of reality about them, despite the fact that we learn nothing about their physical make-up or social connections and history. In fact, these characters, who offer a convincing illusion of reality, are nothing less than stock or stereotype characters whose intertextual origins can be found in classical Greek Literature. For what is the conjurer if he is not the modern version of the EIRON, the trickster figure who undoes the braggart ALAZON (here the Quick Man)?

Irony

IRONY comes from the Greek *eironia*, which meant purposeful ignorance or dissimulation. It always involves at least two levels of meaning (originally the knowing reality concealed behind the feigned ignorance). The most common forms of irony—verbal, situational, dramatic, and irony of events—appear in this text. We immediately confront VERBAL IRONY (see p. 123) when the conjurer opens by saying that he has nothing concealed in the cloth. That emptiness belongs to the world of appearance, the reality of which will be, by the time he has finished his "spiel", that the cloth will contain a goldfish bowl. We meet SITUATIONAL IRONY (see p. 128) when the conjurer gets his revenge and takes the Quick Man's watch and other possessions and actually destroys them while the Quick Man continues to believe that it is all a part of the conjuring act. DRAMATIC IRONY (see p. 128) has two definitions, referring to an outcome the opposite of which was anticipated, or the awareness by the audience or reader of something that a principal character does not know about the inevitable outcome of events. In this text, the title itself informs the reader in advance (prolepsis) that the conjurer will triumph. IRONY OF EVENTS refers to an outcome of events the opposite of what the initiator of those events had intended. Here the Quick Man sets out to disrupt the performance, but gets himself disrupted instead.

Irony and Conjuring

One of the complications of this text with respect to irony is that, whereas in ordinary realist texts informed by dramatic and situational irony a signified "reality" will turn out to have been "appearance" or "illusion", in this text we start out with a context which trades on the play between illusion and reality, for that is what conjuring is about. We know, or believe, that things cannot just disappear in this controlled environment of the conjurer, yet we also know that things will be made to appear and disappear by the conjurer because that is what the discourse of conjuring is about. In an example which does not appear in this text, we know that a beautiful conjurer's assistant will typically appear to have been sawn in half, but in fact will not have been so. In this text the conjurer takes the final step of actually doing the real thing: he actually smashes the watch.

Freytag's Pyramid

Dealing with tragedy and the fate of the hero in 1863, Freytag drew a pyramid, a visual representation of the rise and fall of the hero over the time and space of the text:

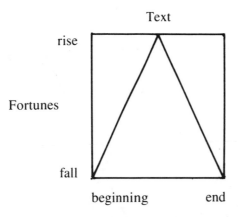

In "The Conjurer's Revenge", this pyramid charts the path of the antagonist, "Quick Man". The Conjurer's fortunes are the reverse of this, the pattern of classical COMEDY:

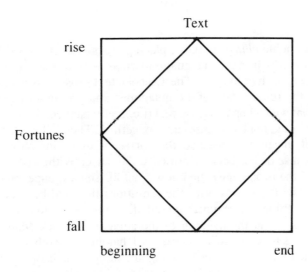

The two patterns brought together produce the following:

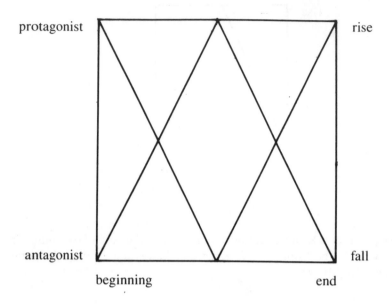

protagonist   rise

antagonist   fall

beginning   end

We may call this a double *chiasmus* (Gk., placing crosswise). CHIASMUS
is a rhetorical figure which causes language to cross over in the following
way: "we eat to live, we live to eat". The Leacock text crosses over in this
fashion to reverse the relationship of the antagonist and protagonist twice.
In the first cross, that which appears to be real (i.e. really happening) actually
does happen so far as the reader's senses are concerned. The reader sees and
hears the defeat of the protagonist and the corresponding triumph of the
antagonist. But because he has been informed at the outset by the title of the
ultimate triumph of the protagonist, he knows that his senses, appearances,
delude him. For while the senses offer the sensations that will become the
"facts" (L. *factum*=thing made) which would allow the reader to construct
a context that would reveal the triumph of the antagonist Quick Man, the
reader knows that he is involved in a process, and that there are other unseen
forces at work which will reverse his winning situation. This happens with
the *peripeteia* (Gk., reversal of fortunes) to produce the following pattern:

184

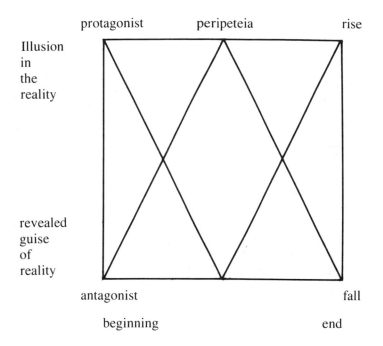

	protagonist	peripeteia	rise
Illusion in the reality			
revealed guise of reality			
	antagonist		fall
	beginning		end

Seeing, Knowing and the Quick Man

The Quick Man receives the sensations that become the data or facts out of which he constructs his understanding of reality: he *knows* this is a trick. His theoretical presuppositions being what they are, his seeing and knowing at the outset produce the apparently correct explanation, with respect to the conjurer, that "He—had—it—up—his—sleeve." What emerges for the reader as the text proceeds, however, is the fact that the Quick Man knows only from within the framework of a naive realist epistemology. From this standpoint there is a static and objective world out there, there is a subject who can use his common sense in order to generate facts out of the sensations received from that objective world, and there is a human language which can name those facts correctly once and for all time. Failing to see that common sense and facts are part of an inadequate philosophy (because he does not believe he either has or needs a philosophy) which takes a static view of a world that is in process, the Quick Man is soon at the mercy of events, for the context of his world changes through an act of will on the part of the conjurer. Trapped by his static naive realist presuppositions, the Quick Man can no longer believe the evidence provided by his senses. His mind tells him that although his watch appears to be smashed, it cannot possibly have been smashed, because that (according to the theory which he does not know he has) cannot happen.

Two Levels of Understanding

The Quick Man, as naive realist, operates on a fixed or homeostatic level of understanding like a thermostat. He cannot understand that we do not "see" with the eyes, but with the mind, and the mind is not inherited from nature, but inscribed by culture. We see through theory (it means "seeing" in Greek), because theory has been built into our structures of perception. The Conjurer, by contrast, operates on a different level of understanding. He operates on the basis of certain theoretical homeorhetic presuppositions that have obviously served him well in practice up to this point. He now meets a practical obstacle which prevents him from working as he has done before. Accordingly, he reflects in the middle of the process, and changes his practice to remove that obstacle. He is praxis in action: practice regulated by theory, and theory adjusted by practice, in a world of morphogenetic process. Here is the intellectual key to this text: Praxis versus practice, process versus statis, that which is the key to survival of the species. The homeostatic mind of the Quick Man is defeated by the morphogenetic leap of mind when the Conjurer turns from tricks to dirty tricks in order to resolve his problem.

Banana Skins

In silent films coming out of vaudeville in the period when "The Conjurer's Revenge" was written, at the beginning of the century, we have the figure of the clown, and we have the banana skin, and we know that the twain must meet. The title of this text is our sight of the banana skin, and the Quick Man is the clown. With our privileged position of superior knowledge, we can laugh while being thankful that we are not the object of laughter. Behind the fun here, though, lies a profound epistemological message.

Harold Pinter's
The Birthday Party

When we reconstruct a story by putting characters and events into linear chronological form, we do not attempt to deal with all the events, only the significant ones. However, the ultimately complete analysis must be capable of answering questions relating to any event or character, whether it has been mentioned or not.

The hermeneutic code plays over the story and through it the author withholds information about characters, places, and events, even as this technique also anticipates characters, places, and events. This manipulation creates a purposeful air of tension that provokes reader interest at the outset and maintains it, if successful, throughout the text.

The process of anticipating events, places and persons we call PROLEPSIS, a particular instance of which we call a PROLEPTIC. A proleptic works PROLEPTICALLY. We meet with prolepsis in the conversation between Meg and Petey in *The Birthday Party* when the proleptic of the car (and wheelbarrow) of Goldberg and McCann proleptically anticipates the arrival of the car. We meet ANALEPSIS later in the play when we discover McCann to be a defrocked priest. This analeptic reaches back analeptically to redefine all we have learned about McCann.

Analepsis and prolepsis operate on the conceptual level of the signified. Signified may refer to the conceptual microcosmic level of the sign or sentence on the one hand, or the macrocosmic level of the text as a whole. Analepsis and prolepsis operate on the macrocosmic level of the text as a whole, not on the microcosmic level of the individual sign. The equivalent of analepsis at the microcosmic level of the sign is CATAPHORA, which means to carry back, while the equivalent of prolepsis is ANAPHORA, which means to carry forward (*ana* in Greek can mean either backwards or forwards).

Whatever else goes on in Pinter's *The Birthday Party*, the play is a battle of generic codes which operate on two distinct levels of discourse. The play opens and closes with all the signs of a classic realist text of the kitchen sink variety. The declining petty bourgeois characters are made to utter their flat and repeated clichés to reveal a completely unreflected and dull life. On this realist level we have an *in medias res* beginning with the promise of a middle and an end. Equilibrium will lead to disequilibrium and then conclude with equilibrium and an affirmation of values and the resolution of the problematic. We do get the equilibrium-disequilibrium-equilibrium sequence, but we do not get any affirmation of values. Indeed, we are never quite sure what values are at stake in this play. Again, while we do get a beginning and an end, the middle is discontinuous and belongs to the discourse of surrealism. Pinter clearly aimed to deconstruct the realist structured minds of theatre-goers in the mid 1950s.

Is *The Birthday Party* Theatre of the Absurd? If by that description we mean the so-called absurdity of modern life (which must mean life as commodity in commodity society) then it by no means follows that Pinter stresses the absurd. He wrote at a time when the retreat from Empire was well under way, a time and process which called for a massive re-evaluation of all spheres of life in his society. With no more natives to kick around, obviously changes had to be made. Meg and Petey represent in this context the massive vulgarity and stupidity of the English petty bourgeoisie, who apparently can learn nothing from experience, cannot even allow that changes have occurred. Stanley is clearly the artist as confusion, hiding from the world of experience and quite prepared to live at the expense of others. Up to this point we are dealing with realist types whose typicality in relation to British society can readily be seen.

McCann and Goldberg are disruptive types of a different order of magnitude. For whereas Meg, Petey and Stanley are univocal types, representing on one easily discernible level a single set of values, McCann and Goldberg are multivocal symbolic types who represent a variety of values, some of them quite incompatible. To deal fully with these characters we would have to disentangle a bewildering mixture of intertextual influences and codes. Intertextually they are on one level very clearly the comic duo of Hollywood thirties films, just as they are also gangster and sidekick from the same source. As an Irish priest McCann represents Christianity, for Ireland was one of the early homes of Christianity, and as a defrocked priest he also represents advanced dechristianized secularism. Goldberg as Jew on this level obviously represents the Hebrew God, but one who has come down to earth in the new secular age. Both also work as ominous agents of the state and other institutions.

The Birthday Party is an interrogative text, as the vast number of questions in it tells us. It is not a declarative or imperative text. That it is interrogative tells us that Pinter does not here view life as absurd, for there is no point in interrogating that which has no meaning. The closest we can come to describing this work is to call it satire, a mirror into which we are supposed to look, see ourselves, and do something about it. Above all, we are supposed to see this play as a construction because it deconstructs itself in front of us. It strips dramatic realism of its illusions in order to shock habituated minds, to break their structures of perception, forcing viewers and readers to see the world anew.

Charles Yale Harrison's
Generals Die In Bed

Generic Code

We do not have to move too far into *Generals Die In Bed* to discern that it fits into the classic realist generic code.

Hermeneutic Code

If the hermeneutic code speaks of the way in which discourse plays across the story, anticipating and holding back information so as to maintain reader interest, then we can see this in action most obviously in the matter of the *Llandovery Castle*. After the General has inspired his troops to fight the hated Huns by telling the soldiers of the atrocity that was the sinking of this hospital ship, our wounded first person narrator discovers that "our" side was illegally using the ship to carry munitions.

The hermeneutic code needs to be followed through in detail, but the incident of the *Llandovery Castle* pushes us in the direction of the cultural codes.

The Two Cultural Codes

Two cultural codes confront each other in this text, and they do so on every level and in every sphere of human experience there. These codes cut across national lines (across enemy lines) to reveal a much more important division along lines of social class between the European imperial establishments, and all the men in the ranks, Germans included.

The Elaborated and Restricted Linguistic Codes

The class lines are not truly clear-cut in this division. On the very first page of the novel, for example, it becomes clear that the first person narrator belongs, by his linguistic code, to the elaborated code of the educated mental worker, and therefore, by definition, should belong on the side of the establishment. He looks on as his fellow recruits of the lower classes (and decidedly restricted linguistic code) return from drinking and whoring. He is an "I" looking at a "them" with no real sense of community (or "we") with them. We shall return later to the "we" community which emerges with the speaker participating in it.

The Two Codes of Heroism

Harrison's novel sets at odds two different kinds of heroism:

a)   the imperialist version of the old knightly code of an arrogant ruling class (both sides);

b)   the low-key heroic code of the oppressed whose heroism amounts to surviving with human dignity the lies, blunders, and inhumanity of a "grand" heroic code which treats them as animals. The shooting of the imperial officer Clark by his own men, and the riot or near revolution, illustrate this.

Religion and the Two Gods

We find a religious code in this novel which sets off the insane patriarchal God of the establishment (the references are numerous) against the ordinary and everyday decency of Mary Magdalene and other figures who tend to the suffering (historical) Christ figures which are the ordinary suffering men.

Two Natures

Nature appears in two forms: that of a nature gone quite mad, and the alternative of a blessed nature renewing itself. In this way, Harrison signifies the decline of the old patriarchal world and the beginnings of a new and more humane democratic order. Animal images help this theme with bombs taking on the characteristics of birds when they are said to "land". This reveals a mad world with culture (bombs) against the organic things (birds) of nature. Sparrows flying freely over the lines indicate the commonality of interest of the ordinary men on both sides.

Two Human Natures

The animal imagery serves to illustrate the reduction of the men to the level of beasts (the rat image particularly), while the other images (the sparrows) speak symbolically of potential human freedom.

Irony and the Title

The title brings out the class division, for when it says *Generals Die In Bed*, it conjures up its opposite and absence, which the text provides, and which we can sum up in the following words: Soldiers Die in Bestial Battle.

Ideological Code

The ideology of the text emerges as decidedly anti-capitalist and pro-socialist. However, Harrison seems not so much concerned with the elimination of capitalism as with the removal of its excesses. The ideology therefore becomes the homeorhetic one of social democracy, with the thorny economic problem left unresolved. We can feel here, though, the kind of anger that just a few years later would produce in Canada the CCF, predecessor of the present NDP. The ideology finally becomes that of populism, with its mixture of individual enterprise and collective caring in a "we" community.

Narration and Story

In *Generals Die In Bed* the narration is simultaneous with the story at the beginning. The speaker speaks:

> It is midnight on pay day. Some of the recruits are beginning to dribble into the barracks bunk room after a night's carousal down the line.

Simple at the signified semantic level, tied by syntax and linear logic, these lines seem to announce themselves as plain prose discourse reportage, dispensing facts. Underneath the signified semantic, however, the signifying system makes clear that this is more than an attempt at an objective, transparent neutrality of style. It speaks of commitment, of a definite and involved (engagé) construction of a view of reality. For example, on the level of signifier the prose draws attention to itself as a medium through the rhyme of "pay/day" and "midnight/night", along with the assonance of "midnight/night/line", "carousal/down", "It/is/midnight/beginning/dribble/ into", and "into/room", not to mention the alliteration of "beginning/barracks/ bunk", "dribble/down", and the hard "K" consonance of "recruits/barracks/ carousal".

The time of the novel is the "now" of the novel, as yet unspecified, but not the "now" of the present day reader. Harrison has his narrator speak to his narrattee in codes that both understand, but these are sufficiently distant from us to make us have to feel our way into the time and the codes.

Some of the events of the story have occurred and so we begin *in medias res*. For if the recruits are beginning to dribble (and note the metaphor), then clearly some have already arrived. We have an equilibrium which will shortly become a disequilibrium. While the speaker here appears as spectator, he soon reveals himself as a participant in the events. Being a first person narrator, he cannot be an omniscient third person narrator. He cannot be God.

Narratorical and Ideological Position

Were the narrator to be a third person and like a God, Harrison would have created an irreconcilable contradiction in his text between a privileged third person narrator and his democratic populist ideology, which refuses to recognize privileged positions.

Double Significatum

In the opening lines of *Generals Die In Bed* Harrison writes of "down the line" and quickly adds that:

> Down the line in Montreal is Cadieux St., St. Elizabeth St....

But "down the line" has already invoked the military code to proleptically anticipate action down the front line in France where the men will soon be. This creates a parallel:

Stressing the low-key heroic, Harrison wants to draw attention to the scruffy dress and seedy morals of the men and pose them against the well-dressed, "civilized" manner of the establishment. He widens the gap between these two, and plays on the popular establishment view of the men as beasts (whores, booze), but prepares us, with the military meaning, for the anticipation of France. He prepares for the dialectical twist the text will take when the men become civilized and the officer caste become anti-human beings, and so on. This process has its sequel in the novel with the incident of the *Llandovery Castle* already referred to.

Pronouns and Community

Let us examine the scene in which the old French peasant and the narrator-speaker meet:

"Tabac?" he asks.

Here we have an example of ellipsis, for the real question is: "Do you have any pipe tobacco, sir?" The question is an interrogation, but made by a supplicant in no position of power to ask favours, and therefore it gets asked with hesitation.

The direct discourse reveals the other as a "he", a third person other, nominative case. "He" is a subject, viewed as an object, and "other", without a name.

The verb "asks" derives from the Anglo-Saxon verb *ascian*. An intransitive verb, it here appears in its third person singular present tense. "He" and "asks" therefore stress the singularity of the "other".

"I hesitate."

The first person singular nominative case pronoun, the "I", stresses the separate ego, this other of the "he" in this situation.

The first person present tense of the verb "hesitate" derives from the Latin (*haesitare*=to stick fast, to stop or pause respecting a decision).

"One is not generous in war."

The hesitation leads to a shift away from the other as indicated by the impersonal pronoun "one". Given a choice between entering into an I-thou relationship of friendship or an I-it relationship of power, the "one" indicates a tendency towards I-it, a relationship of distance and objectification.

The verb "is" serves as a connective verb, the third person singular of the verb "to be". This third person verb is a verb form appropriate to the "he", not to this "I" (I am), and the use of "one is" thus helps to indicate the impersonality of the speaker, to reveal himself setting up a defensive-aggressive power relationship of the I-it kind with the old man. The negative "not" clearly introduces a negative element, and this negativity is reinforced by the root meaning of "generous". This sign has its origins in the Latin (*generosus*=of good and noble birth). The speaker will not have nobility of spirit.

The preposition "in" expresses inclusion with relation to space, time, state, circumstances, manner, quality substance, a class, a whole, etc. "In" prepares for "war" which comes from the Old High German (*werre*=confusion, strife).

> The open armed conflict between nations or states, or between parties in the same state carried on by force of arms between hostile parties...[*O.E.D*]

Here, of course, we have conflict both between the Germans and the Allies, and between the troops and their officers in the imperial establishment.

> "His eyes beseech me."

"His eyes": third person singular, possessive (the other as possessive). Metonymy here has eyes standing as part of the whole of his person. This visual gesture produces the idea of the eyes as windows of the soul to suggest that he is a being (thou) with a soul.

"beseech": "be", an Anglo-Saxon prefix as intensifier; *sechen* (Anglo-Saxon, to seek). This is the entreaty of a supplicant with the religious implication of a mortal praying to a transcendent God.

"me": leaves us still with the speaker as object in an I-it relationship through the objective first person pronoun.

The verb "beseech" acts on the object "me" to produce the transformation and the speaker's essential goodness.

> I gave him my pouch.

The "I" gives another objective-object "him" a possessive "my pouch", a piece of property.

> He takes his blackened pipe.

We are still with the third person other with his own property, "his blackened pipe".

We smoke in silence.

The "we" completes the sequence with "community" established. The "I" and "he" have now merged. Smoke and silence alliterate to suggest a unity of sounds in the process. As a Canadian novel with implication of Canadian Indians and the origin of tobacco in North America, we have the pipe of peace and community set off against the background of war.

We see how character, action, story and ideology operate as discourse plays over story in the scene where the speaker in *Generals Die In Bed* meets the Anglican curate in London. At that point he is on leave and living with the kind-hearted whore (a term that becomes meaningless in this context). Let us call the Anglican curate A and the speaker B.

(B) As I come out, an Anglican curate sees my listless face. It is wartime and no introductions are necessary.
[The social class codes have been relaxed to allow people to meet each other in a way that was not possible before the war.]

(A) "Hello."
[A speaks from the position of privilege and rank, even if he is friendly.]

(B) "Hello."
[Note that the speaker does not respect the cultural code that has not been relaxed. B does not say, "Hello, Sir", "Hello, Padre", etc. He speaks as an equal.]

(A) "You look tired."
[A still takes the initiative in the conversation which means that he wishes to establish the code in terms of which the discourse will proceed.]

(B) "Yes."
[The speaker still resists falling into the code of the other.]

(A) "On leave?"
[Undeterred, the curate still responds. Neither side has given way yet in this silent war of words.]

(B) "Yes, going back tomorrow."
[Still does not indicate any submission.]

(A) "Itching to get back I'll wager."

(B) "I'll be itching when I get back."

With these last two lines the two codes of the hierarchical curate and the egalitarian speaker hit head-on with the sign "itching". Oxford offers two basic meanings of "itch":

1) An uneasy sensation of irritation in the skin, specially a contagious disease, in which the skin is covered with vesicles and pustules, accompanied by extreme irritation, now known to be produced by the itch mite.
2) (figurative meaning). An uneasy or restless hankering after something.

The curate uses itching in the second metaphorical sense, being careful not to note the physical, pathological definition. A man of the spirit, A thinks in abstract spiritual terms. The narrator quickly spots this, recognizes the situational irony, and inserts the physical definition to lower the conversation to that of the level of life in the trenches, so as to force the curate either to leave or continue the conversation on his terms.

The curate enters the verbal codes of the narrator with the nervous, humorous: "Ha, ha, that *is* a good one—you'll be itching *after* you get back. I must remember that one."

Working Through a Complete Text: "Sylvie", a Post-Modern Text by David Arnason

The Text

(1) Sylvie says she loves me, but I believe she lies. (2) She hasn't been to see me since the last day in July. (3) That would be the thirty-first, and here it is into September. (4) I know it's a busy season, all that cotton to pick, all them bales to tote, but you'd think she could bring me a little water every little once in a while. (5) I don't think it's asking too much as a proof of love.

(6) Sylvie claims she's been out of town, modelling in front of fountains in Rome, sitting on the walls of ruined castles along the Rhine, dressed in the newest styles. (7) Tweeds are in, she tells me. (8) There's a fortune to be made in tweeds. (9) Put all your money into tweeds. (10) What about cotton, I ask her, what about her Mammy and her Pappy and all her brothers and sisters down there in good ol' Alabam. (11) Cotton's out, she says. (12) Pappy, that slackass old bastard, ain't gonna make a penny on cotton. (13) It's gonna be a lean winter down on the farm, now that tweed is in.

(14) Pappy's been complaining about the moonshine, I tell her. (15) He's been sending me letters complaining he can't get no moonshine. (16) Sylvie says she sent him a gallon of Remy Martin. (17) He just pigs it down, she says. (18) Them people live like animals, she says. (19) You can't do nuthin for them.

(20) Sylvie phones me from Paris. (21) She's modelling tweeds on the left bank. (22) I'm dying for water, I tell her. (23) Bring me little water, Sylvie, I say. (24) You got running water, she tells me. (25) Get yourself a glass and walk on over to the kitchen sink. (26) Sylvie says she loves me. (27) This can't be true, I tell her. (28) If she really loved me, she'd have come and see me. (29) I point out that she hasn't been to see me since the last day in July. (30) I got a job, she says. (31) I'm a working girl. (32) We'll spend the Christmas holidays skiing at Banff.

(33) I dream of Sylvie. (34) I dream of Sylvie in my arms, Sylvie bringing me water. (35) Sylvie doesn't dream of me. (36) She says she can't dream. (37) I say she could dream if she wanted, it's not that she can't dream, she won't dream. (38) I want to be in Sylvie's dreams. (39) I tell her if she just gives me a chance, I'll be wonderful in her dreams. (40) I'll bring her pleasure free from guilt. (41) I've promised if she dreams of me I'll take her to verdant glades. (42) Sylvie says there weren't no verdant glades back in old Alabam. (43) Nuthin but them old cotton fields back home.

(44) I've sent Sylvie two heart-shaped lockets. (45) One is blue and says *All Love Sylvie*. (46) The other's red and says *Sylvie Loves All*. (47) I got her two eighteen-carat gold chains to hang them around her neck. (48) I told her I was so hot and dry that a little drink of water wouldn't satisfy me. (49) Sylvie sent me a postcard from Copenhagen. (50) The picture showed Sylvie in tweed posing in front of a fountain. (51) She said she loved me. (52) I'm not sure she's telling the truth. (53) She hasn't been to see me since the last day in July.

(54) I've got this tune running through my head. (55) It goes, "Oh for Friday nicht, Friday's lang a-coming." (56) That's all I can remember. (57) There's got to be more words but I can't think of them. (58) If Sylvie were here, she'd know them. (59) She knows the words to all the songs. (60) I run down to the supermarket and buy all the ladies' magazines. (61) They all have pictures of Sylvie dressed in tweeds, posing in front of water fountains. (62) Little drink of water, wouldn't satisfy me.

(63) Kissing Sylvie is the best thing. (64) Sylvie has a wonderful mouth. (65) The first time she kissed me, we were only friends saying goodbye. (66) Her mouth was red and sweet, and fresh. (67) I couldn't think of anything else for days. (68) The next time I kissed her, I asked her to marry me. (69) Sylvie said she loved me, but she wouldn't marry me, only because she was already married.

(70) Sylvie likes sandwiches, those little cocktail sandwiches that you pop into your mouth whole. (71) She loves chocolates, the round sweet ones with a cherry in the centre. (72) She pops them into her mouth. (73) She drinks from long straws, pursing her mouth and looking up at you with wide open eyes. (74) Sylvie pops raspberries and strawberries into her mouth. (75) She bites deeply into peaches and pears, and doesn't care if the juice drips. (76) She

bites into the red skin of apples and the orange flesh of oranges. (77) Her kisses are sweet.

(78) Sylvie sends me a telegram from Scotland. (79) She says she is posing in tweeds in front of waterfalls. (80) She has seen her husband, she says. (81) That sucker isn't worth a pinch of peppered coonshit, she tells me. (82) Sylvie says she loves me. (83) She will be home Friday. (84) I send Sylvie a telegram. (85) I tell her, Oh for Friday nicht, Friday's lang a-coming. (86) Bring me little water, Sylvie. (87) Every little once in a while.

(88) Sylvie's Pappy phones me up. (89) We done run out of moonshine, boy, he tells me. (90) Sure is hot down on them cotton fields without any moonshine. (91) That Remy Martin weren't hardly enough to raise a thirst. (92) I send him a gallon of Dewar's Ne Plus Ultra. (93) I pass on Sylvie's message. (94) Get out of cotton, old man. (95) Tweed is in. (96) Put all your money into tweed.

(97) Sylvie phones me from Newfoundland. (98) She's posing in tweeds on a fishing boat out in them old squid jigging grounds. (99) She's a little tipsy from drinking screech. (100) Put them fishermen in a cotton field, she says, and you couldn't tell the difference. (101) That screech is great moonshine, she says. (102) She's sending a gallon to her Pappy. (103) I tell her she hasn't been to see me since the last day in July. (104) I'll be home on Friday, she says.

(105) I dream of Sylvie with her black, black hair, her black, black eyes. (106) Sylvie doesn't dream of me. (107) Let me into your dreams, I tell her. (108) I'm a good man in a dream. (109) I'm kind and gentle. (110) I can bring you joy. (111) Sorry, Sylvie says, I can't dream. (112) I think she could dream if she wanted to. (113) I believe she lies.

(114) Sylvie's coming on Friday nicht, but Friday's lang a-coming. (115) I'm getting ready. (116) I've bought her peaches and cherries, strawberries and raspberries, oranges and bright red apples. (117) I've bought her ice cream and syrup and long thin straws so she can look up at me with her eyes wide open. (118) I've bought her large bright cotton bibs, so the juice of peaches and pears won't drip on her tweed suit. (119) I've bought her paper napkins with pictures of elves on them, so she can wipe her mouth when she's through. (120) I've bought her a new heart-shaped locket with an eighteen-carat gold chain. (121) When you look at it from a distance, it's blue, but when you look at it close up, it's red.

(122) Sylvie says she loves me. (123) Tomorrow will be Friday, and Sylvie's coming home. (124) I'll kiss her in the airport, and I'll kiss her in the taxi and I'll feed her strawberries when we get home. (125) Tonight I'll dream about her, and maybe she'll dream about me. (126) I'm a good man in a dream. (127) Bring me little water, Sylvie. (128) I'll feed you raspberries and peaches and pears. (129) You can drink from a long thin straw and look up at me from your wide, black eyes. (130) Bring it in a bucket, Sylvie. (131) Bring it in a bucket, now.

Critique

The idea of a plot or *mythos* (Gk., story) with a beginning, a middle, and an end, a complete action of the right order of magnitude in literary *mimesis* (Gk., imitation, representation) of reality comes from Aristotle (384-322 B.C.) and his *Poetics*, a theoretical study based on his analysis of Greek literature, especially tragedy. The poet (Gk. *poet*=maker) constructs a literary object and Aristotle reveals a desire to understand how the object gets made, and to what purpose.

Habituation to the basic principles of the closed realist text has now led some to the very misleading view that somehow the literary construct exists in a one-to-one relationship with life in the empirical world. It does not, of course, because life does not have the relatively clean linear lines of a realist text, and neither does it conclude with the end of an action and the affirmation of value. Realism, then, before it is "real" or anything else, consists of a set of conventions. It is one way of talking about the world through literary discourse, but not the only one. This we shall see with Arnason's "Sylvie".

Victorian Fetishism

The Victorians—by which is meant the Victorian bourgeoisie—made a fetish of realist plots which closed and completed their action with an affirmation of value (F. *fetiche*=sorcery, witchcraft; L. *factitius*=artifical, from *facio*=to make, the whole thing coming to mean an object of superstitious awe or worship). The reaction against these plots in the twentieth century is:

a)   partly a revolt against the dead hand of a realist theory which easily becomes mere technique;

b)   partly a means of disrupting readers' minds and dislocating their structures of perception from the habituation to realist texts, an habituation which makes them seem totally "real";

c)   partly a consequence of the problematic nature of twentieth-century life in which the more we know, the less we seem to know, somehow or other;

d)   partly an accommodation of the fact that along with the theoretical splitting of the atom at the beginning of the century came the splitting, by Freud, of the old bourgeois ego, to reveal some subconscious dimensions to human experience in modern mass society that the old realist literary conventions could not handle.

Among those Victorians who were aware that the world was not as it seemed to be, who knew that illusion could be reality and reality illusion, was Lewis Carroll of *Alice in Wonderland* fame. It is for this reason that Arnason took some concepts from Carroll's *Bruno and Sylvie* as a starting point for his text, "Sylvie".

In Medias Res

"Sylvie" begins *in medias res* (L., in the middle of things) with the clause: "Sylvie says she loves me..." These words appear out of silence to assert the existence, nature, and beginning of the process that will establish the text. We are so completely habituated to this kind of beginning through reading realist texts that we take it for a fact of nature, for the real, rather than for a convention of culture.

Syntagma

The linear, horizontal progression of the noun/verb/pronoun/verb/pronoun sequence on an apparently single syntactical and semantic level establishes the first sentence as superpositional thought, plain prose discourse, or what *seems* to be the typical neutral, transparent, objective conveyer of meaning that plain prose discourse strives for.

Denotation and Connotation

The signs in this first sequence of six words seem to be denotative rather than connotative:

a) DENOTATION. 1532 (L., *denotationem*)
   (i)   The action of denoting, expression by marks, signs or symbols....
   (ii) A designation (1631)
   (iii) The signification of a term (1614)
   (iv) Logic: that which a word *denotes* as distinct from its *connotation*.
                                                          [*O.E.D.*]

b) CONNOTATION. 1532 (L., *connotationem*)
   (i)   The signifying in addition; inclusion of something in the meaning of a word besides what it primarily denotes; implication.
   (ii) Logic: the attribute or attributes connoted by a term....[*O.E.D.*]

In denotation, the signifying system seeks to call up precise concepts in both its individual signifieds and in their mutual relationships within the syntactical unit. This leaves no space for the reader to interpolate thoughts and feelings other than those prescribed by the text. By contrast, a connotative line would have a looseness in the relationship between signifiers and signifieds, as well as between them in the syntactical unit, so as to encourage the reader to interpolate a certain range of other meanings and signifieds into the text.

Beginnings, Middles, and Ends

The precise linear flow of the whole first sentence suggests that this text will be a realist text, and that what we experience in this sentence ("Sylvie says she loves me, but I believe she lies") is the first part of the three-part macro-structure common to such texts with a beginning, a middle, and an end.

Closure

In fact, we are prepared for a process that will not only proceed through a beginning to a middle and an end, but will be brought to an end through CLOSURE, to somehow round out the whole action, to conclude with a satisfactory resolution of the problematic of the work and an affirmation of some set of values that have been imperilled in the conflict of the text.

We shall see that "Sylvie" has closure without any resolution of the problematic, a closure on the level of the signifying system rather than the signified.

Parataxis

The **PARATACTIC** text does not proceed through a linear logic. Consider the following sentences:

> The cat padded in, stopped, saw the mouse, and proceeded to stalk it.
> I came, I saw, I conquered.

In the first sentence we follow a linear logic which unfolds step by step without requiring anything beyond a kind of passive attention on our part as we follow it through. The second set of signs is different. As Easthope puts it in his *Poetry as Discourse*:

> Traditionally, parataxis is distinguished from syntaxis: while Caesar's "I came, I saw, I conquered" is paratactic, its equivalent in syntaxis would be something like "After I had come and seen, then I conquered". Laird [*The Singer of Tales*, 1960] claims that

oral poetry selects prefabricated formulaic units and sets them alongside each other in paratactic combinatons....

Pei and Gaynor in *Dictionary of Linguistics* define parataxis as:

The coordination or juxtapostion of two or more phrases of equal rank or significance.

As with phrases, so with the larger units that constitute the text "Sylvie". Rather than the superpositional logic of a "when...then...then" series in, say, a Shakespearean sonnet, "Sylvie" works more like a juxtapositional traditional ballad (typically paratactic), being linked not so much through the ordering of concepts in logical sequence at the level of signified conceptual meaning, as by the repetition of different sets of material signifiers and their variants, such as: "a little water every little once in a while", "Tweeds in", "Cotton", "lockets", "last day in July", and so on.

More on Closure

In the text, closure takes place at the level of the signifier without resolving the problematic at the level of the signified. Arnason does this by bringing together in original and variant forms the repetitions and refrain-like utterances scattered throughout the text. To close the text off, leaving us satisfied that it has come to an end, while yet leaving the text ideologically open-ended, Arnason breaks the rule of not introducing new material into a conclusion when he concludes "Bring it in a bucket, now."

Equilibrium-Disequilibrium-Equilibrium

This beginning, middle, and end of the realist text involves a conflict between different value sets to produce the equilibrium-disequilibrium-equilibrium sequence. In "Sylvie" we start with the equilibrium of:

Sylvie says she loves me....

Because the whole text runs to only about 1250 words, it must quickly move to disequilibrium, and that it does with the second clause of the compound introductory sentence:

Sylvie says she loves me, but I believe she lies.

The adversative conjunction or disjunction "but" (but I on the other hand believe...) produces a quick VOLTA (L. *volvere*=to turn) or turn in thought to destroy the conceptual equilibrium established by the first clause.

"Sylvie" proceeds, then, from equilibrium to disequilibrium, but we shall see that it does not establish a new conceptual equilibrium at the end.

The Opposing Literary Code

The realist sentences of the plain prose discourse make perfect linear sense. This cannot be said of the following typical lines:

> Sylvie phones me from Paris. She's modelling tweeds on the left bank. I'm dying for water, I tell her. Bring me little water, Sylvie, I say. You got running water, she tells me. Get yourself a glass and walk on over to the kitchen sink.

The absence of semantic common sense here contrasts with the clean linearity of the syntax of these normative sentences to introduce, through the strange logic, an alternative literary code.

Disruption

"Sylvie" seems to establish itself swiftly as a realist text in a couple of sentences, to set all the reader's habituations and assumptions into place. It then proceeds to disrupt those expectations. Arnason does this in order to bring into question the "reality" of so-called realist prose discourse. He accomplishes his goal in two ways: the first is obvious in passages like the one above, which disrupt the linear progress of plain prose discourse; the second one is not initially obvious: we find this in the disruptive tendencies of the signifying system of the first, "realist", sentence itself.

Antithetical Parallelism

Before we bracket the signified of the first sentence we need to note the implications of the turn in thought raised by the adversative conjunction "but":

> . Sylvie says she loves me, but I believe she lies.

This makes the sentence a classical example of antithetical parallelism, parallel because the two clause units are perfectly balanced with six syllables each:

> Sylvie says she loves me,
> but I believe she lies.

Each has a single two-syllable sign and four single-syllable signs. The clause units are antithetical because semantically the clauses oppose one another (Gk. *anti*=opposite, against; *thesis*=proposition, affirmation; an opposition or contrast of ideas). The first sentence is a microcosm of the macrocosmic text because the text itself is an antithetical parallel text.

Signifiers as Language

Behind the turn in thought that produced the antithetical parallelism of the first sentence, a lot of interesting things are going on among the signifiers. First, we note the medial (middle) and terminal (end) juncture (pause) which divides the compound sentence down the middle.

Sylvie says she loves me / but I believe she lies. //

Rhythm

Then we reach the interesting rhythm:

/ ‿ / ‿ / ‿ ‿ / ‿/ ‿ /
Sylvie says she loves me / but I believe she lies.

Here a trochaic (loud/soft [/ ‿]) trimeter (three measures of feet having two beats each) first clause, opposes an iambic (soft/loud [‿ /]) trimeter second clause. Since iambic metre has been the dominant metre in the English language, it becomes here the norm which defines negatively, on the level of rhythm, the first trochaic trimeter clause, its opposite. It therefore defines Sylvie by negation. The rhythm secretly privileges the iambic speaker over the trochaic Sylvie, even as it makes the two oppose each other.

Alliteration and Foregrounding

Alliteration (repetition of the initial consonant sounds) links the ''s'' phoneme to Sylvie by foregrounding it through repetition against the background of diverse unpatterned phonemes:

Sylvie says she...she...

This ''s'' phoneme when repeated produces a hissing effect. This hissing has the conventional stigma of the snake attached to it in Judeo-Christian culture, for it is associated with the biblical Eve figure. And so it is used here to signify Sylvie negatively as an Eve figure. Meanwhile, the alliteration of ''loves'' and "lies" foregrounds these two signs against the background of the diverse other sounds to create a kind of infra-oxymoron (Gk., *oxus*=sharp; *moros*=dull, foolish; joined contradictory signs designed to give point to a statement). The signs "loves" and "lies" neatly sum up the ambiguous relationship of the narrator and Sylvie in anticipation of the narrative to come. This makes "loves" and "lies" proleptics (Gk. *prolepsis*=anticipation).

Assonance and Foregrounding

We have similar foregrounding through assonance (repetition of similar vowel sounds), and to the same effect, with

> Sh<u>e</u> m<u>e</u> bel<u>ie</u>ve sh<u>e</u>

Yet the assonance "<u>I</u>" "<u>lie</u>s", linking "I" with the third person "she lies", proleptically anticipates the characteristic *third person relationship* that the text as a whole will present. Also, the objective first person pronoun "me" and its assonantal connection with the third person "she" similarly anticipates his treatment, by her, as "object" in return.

Consonance and Foregrounding

The consonance achieved through the repeated "v" phonemes "lo<u>v</u>es" and "belie<u>v</u>e" joins the two to suggest a positive view of the relationship, but this gets unmistakably undermined by the consonance of the "l" sounds which foreground "Sy<u>l</u>vie", "<u>l</u>oves", and "<u>l</u>ies".

Near-Rhyme and Foregrounding

Adding to the negative view is the foregrounded near-rhyme of [Sylvie] "say<u>s</u>", "love<u>s</u>" and "lie<u>s</u>".

Readerly and Writerly Text

Were the text of "Sylvie" to proceed monologically in the linear fashion of the first clause, we would undoubtedly have a "readerly" text; as Roland Barthes calls it, a massaging text. A readerly text has its opposite in a writerly text, a messaging text. In a readerly text the language facilitates the reading so that through familiarity with classic literature, or works written in classic style, the reading process is not disturbed or disrupted by the language. The "writerly" or messaging text deliberately draws attention to its language to make language a main issue in the text. This first "Sylvie" clause appears at first to be in readerly form and to promise a readerly text. In fact, we end up getting a battle between readerly and writerly texts to make this a writerly text in which the text draws attention to the difference between these two types of texts.

Story and Discourse

HISTOIRE (story) means the simple linear chronology of events to which a realist text can be reduced. DISCOURSE plays over the STORY to produce the TEXT. Through anticipation or prolepsis (see p. 187), the text can make us look forward to an event, or with flashback or analepsis (see p. 187), it can make us look back to some event which has been withheld from us. By these and other means the author keeps our interest in his text open until we reach the end.

In the typical realist text with its beginning, middle and end, we can usually gather together somewhat easily the significant features which constitute the story. That proves by no means to be an easy task with "Sylvie". This text, by being a writerly text, presents itself as predominantly discourse.

Monology and Dialogy

Realist texts are by definition monological because their beginning, middle and end, equilibrium, disequilibrium and final equilibrium, lead to an affirmation of a single vision, a single set of values, a single voice. In the dialogical text, a number of voices and values, some of them alien to the author's own voice and values, get free expression and are, finally, neither affirmed nor denied. In "Sylvie", we cannot really tell whether the author or narrator behind the speaker denies the values of the speaker and Sylvie, or just makes the speaker speak without comment. While there is no certainty about denial, the text most assuredly does not affirm their values, or any others.

Menippean Satire

Menippus was an ancient Greek philosopher and satirist whose works have been lost, but whose general form of discourse has not. MENIPPEAN DISCOURSE has no respect for the linearity of the realist text, nor does it have any sense of decorum. DECORUM refers to a certain appropriateness of behaviour as determined by the rules of polite society. Decorum in eighteenth-century polite society, for example, forbade (except in satire) the use of the sign "fish" and insisted on such circumlocutions as "finny tribe".

Menippean discourse is irreverent, bawdy, deflating, disrupting, and may move with ease from church to whorehouse, from gravity to carnival. "Sylvie" has all these general Menippean characteristics.

Intertextuality

In order to deny the romantic myth of the untutored genius-writer who invents *ex nihilo* (L., out of nothing) his universe like God, structuralism insists that every text is an INTERTEXT, the meeting point of many texts which have influenced the writer, whether he knows it or not. Take the first sentence:

> Sylvie says she loves me, but I believe she lies.

When Arnason wrote this he had in the back of his mind the popular song sung by Harry Belafonte, which it repeats in clear prose form, and Lewis Carroll's large prose text *Bruno and Sylvie*. Arnason was not conscious of the Shakespeare influence (though he knows Shakespeare well).

> When my love swears that she is made of truth
> I do believe her, though I know she lies,

What we have in "Sylvie", then, is a conscious use of intertextuality, along with unconscious influences. The end of the second sentence "last day in July" clearly recalls the Leadbelly song. In sentence (4) "all that cotton to pick, all them bales to tote" takes us straight to Paul Robeson and "Ol' Man River". In the same sentence, "bring me little water" conjures up Belafonte again with the song which goes "Bring me little water Sylvie / every little once in a while." The sign "proof" in sentence (6) draws on legal discourse, while "in front of fountains" is a visual cliché from advertising. The phrase "good ol Alabam" sounds like something from popular music.
  Sentence (33) "I dream of Sylvie" recalls Stephen Foster's "I dream of Jeannie with the light brown hair", until we get disrupted in this line by Sylvie. The phrase "old cotton fields back home" again brings in popular music (42) while the two lockets (44-46) come from Carroll's "Bruno and Sylvie". "Oh for Friday nicht" has its origins in an old Scottish song near the beginning of "Bruno and Sylvie". The gustatory sequences (70-77) have their inspiration in the Carroll text. "I dream of Sylvie with her black, black hair..." (105) most obviously recalls the Stephen Foster song again, and so on.

Declarative, Interrogative, Imperative Texts

Just as there are three basic kinds of sentences representing the three fundamental ways in which we deal with each other (declarative = statement,

209

interrogative=question, and imperative=command), so are texts typically one, the other, or combinations of these. In terms of actual questions, the text "Sylvie" has only one of them, and even there the question mark has been left out. Nor are there more than a few imperatives, the great part of the sentences being declarative. If we simply count the number and style of sentences, we would have to call this a declarative text. Because the whole work comes out of an ironic vision, however, this text becomes an interrogative one by drawing into question the values of the narrator and his whole world.

Pronouns: Individual and Community

The narrator uses the name "Sylvie" thirty-three times in the 1250 or so words, but that, of course, tells us nothing, except that the character has such a name. The name tells us nothing about the person. Apart from the actions (the trivial surface media-existence of posing in front of fountains) the character of the relationship between the two personàe does, however, tell us something about her. This is supposed to be a love relationship, because she says she loves him (or so he tells us), but he thinks she lies. A love relationship means a union of two, and grammatically a union of two calls for the use of the first person plural pronoun "we". Yet, the sign "we" appears only twice, along with the sign "we'll", which also appears only twice. Not much community or love here.

The first "we'll" appears in sentence (32): "We'll spend the Christmas holidays skiing at Banff." Whether the narrator uses "we'll" here, or whether Sylvie does, we cannot know, because of ambiguity. If we look back a few sentences, we see the problem:

> I point out that she hasn't been to see me since the last day in July.
> I got a job, she says. I'm a working girl. We'll spend the Christmas
> holidays skiing at Banff.

Is he still speaking for Sylvie, or is he speaking from his own side? The confusion begins to suggest what we know to be true: the "we" has no centre. There is no "we" or community.

Narratorical "Intrusions"

Arnason sets up his speaker as a self-sufficient character in a dramatic monologue who reveals himself by what he says. The author as puppet master disappears behind the character to pull off a confidence trick. Actually this is only apparently so, however, because through his manipulation of the signifying system the author reveals his absent presence to us. For example,

210

the three sentences "(108) I'm a good man in a dream. (109) I'm kind and gentle. (110) I can bring you joy" work in the context where they appear, but apply equally as well on a different level of signification to the author himself—a kind and gentle man who brings joy through his art.

Irony

Irony moves in all directions within this work. The speaker says:

> Sylvie says she loves me, but I believe she lies.

He does not say "know she lies", but "believe she lies". We do not get too far into the text before we *know* that either a) Sylvie does not love him and she lies; or b) we would not recognize, could not recognize, that she loved him, even if she did. From what he says, and from the way in which Arnason makes him say it, we know more than he does. We, therefore, have a SITUATIONAL IRONY in which things are the opposite of what the speaker *really* believes: that Sylvie does love him. We follow the sustained irony through the text in the manner of the irony structured into a play, and thus this is a form of DRAMATIC IRONY. It could be that Sylvie loves him, despite her life of surface media glamour, despite appearances, and that would be ironical. It could also be that, ironically, he does not really believe it when he says she lies, yet ironically she does lie, her words being VERBAL IRONY, meaning the opposite of what she says, and her *situation* being ironical because it is the opposite of what it appears to be. Anything is possible in Menippean discourse.

Character as Simple Types

Within the limited space of about 1250 words we get an imprecisely clear sense of the three main characters as simple types of man, woman, and father figures.

Character as Religious Types

The "s" sounds in the first sentence easily suggest an Eve figure. Eve implies Adam, the pair imply a God, and the fact that there are three figures supports this view of the work. Interestingly, this God may be a black God who drinks moonshine (we never learn his colour). This is quite in keeping with Menippean discourse.

Character as Stereotype

In the early nineteenth century, stereotype (Gk. *stereus*=solid, *typos*=type) meant a cast plate used in printing multiple copies. These characters are all cast plates whose copies we can find in the media (advertising and models, films and southern sheriffs: "boy").

Character as Lukacsian Types

In his *The Intellectual Physiognomy of Literary Character* the Hungarian Marxist philosopher Lukacs delineates his concept of the great "realist" types. Lukacs demonstrates that all the great realist characters in literature are great and convincing not because of their individuality, but because of their typicality. By this he means that these characters are not individuals who hold philosophical views, but individuals as exemplary models of specific philosophical views; characters of depth who *are* and live their views. The truly great ones will embody the major tendencies of the age. These Arnason characters perfectly sum up what Dorothy Parker said when she remarked of someone: "Deep down he is a very shallow man." Deep down these are very shallow people, and they perfectly embody the depthless shallows of a commodity consuming society.

The Enounced and the Enunciation

The speaker in "Sylvie" speaks of certain events. This process has two sides to it: the events themselves, and the verbal utterance which constitutes these events in discourse. The events we call the ENOUNCED, the speaking about them we call the ENUNCIATON. Both the enounced and the enunciation have subjects. The subject of the enounced for the speaker is Sylvie. On that level, the narrator is the subject of the enunciation; i.e., he hears what he says or thinks, or sees what he writes or has written.

As we pick up this text and start to read it, *we become the subject of the enunciation*, the ones who will decode or interpret the text. But in this process certain changes occur so that the subject of the enounced is no longer Sylvie, but Sylvie only in the context of her relations with the speaker. In his world of isolated and alienated individualism, the speaker focuses on one individual as the vehicle for his philosophical position. We, however, see his position, and we are, as the subjects of the enunciation, invited to see this as a relationship (with all the implications of potential community) in two senses: first, that the relationship seems clearly to be inadequate as a genuine expression of love; secondly, by implying community through the false community of the two, the text calls up the *absent* authentic community which, though not specified, serves to condemn the world as it is presented here (without affirming any other). This is the central structural or situational irony of the work: the calling up, by the present false community of the two, a series of notions of authentic community.

Had this been a typical realist text it would have assumed a passive reader whose "ego" it would proceed to "massage" and affirm. This text does not allow that linear kind of process, and it makes the matter of the ego the problematic of the text, when it sets out to disrupt the subject of the enunciation, the reader, by making him check his own sense of self against that of these characters.

Kenosis

This term comes from the Greek and has a traditional theological meaning. It defines an idealist self-emptying process and refers to the way in which spirit can drain itself away from matter. However, it may be used metaphorically to describe the drained-out state of an exhausted society which has lost its sense of mission, structure, and coherence, and is without depth. This is what we meet in "Sylvie".

Space Time

Of the 131 sentences in "Sylvie", eighty-five have verbs which focus on the present, nineteen on the past, nine on the past-present axis, seven on the past-future, and seven on the future. The question, of course, is not simply one of past, present and future.

The mention in the second and third sentences of July and September introduces the theme of the seasons of nature:

> She hasn't been to see me since the last day in July. That would
> be the thirty-first, and here it is into September.

This speaks of the height of summer and the beginnings of fall, but does so through the resonating lines of popular song, which places the speaker already at one remove from nature. The theme of seasons gets reinforced in sentence (4):

> I know it's a busy season, all that cotton to pick, all them bales
> to tote, but you'd think she could bring me a little water every
> little once in a while.

Water and crop clearly conjures up the seasons. The speaker utters these words with irony, however, to distinguish himself from nature, seasons, and the organic. As an urban type, he joins Sylvie, who has left the rural world of seasons and also distances herself from that world and its values, as sentences (17) to (19) demonstrate:

> He [Pappy] just pigs it [brandy] down, she says. Them people live like animals, she says. You can't do nuthin for them.

The metaphor "pigs" says everything about her distance from the rural world and its time-code of the seasons, its planting, growing and harvesting.

Sylvie inhabits the quite different urban time code of fashion, which contrasts with the rural code. Time is a measure of events as process, and this we can see quite clearly with the cyclical progression of the seasons. The time of fashion is irrational, unpredictable, and devastating for those following the traditional rural way of life. This we learn in sentences (7) to (13):

> Tweeds are in, she tells me. There's a fortune to be made in tweeds. Put all your money into tweeds. What about cotton, I ask her, what about her Mammy and her Pappy and all her brothers and sisters down there in good ol' Alabam. Cotton's out, she says. Pappy, that slackass old bastard, ain't gonna make a penny on cotton. It's gonna be a lean winter down on the farm, now that tweed is in.

This is an abstract world in which money (an abstraction) goes out into an abstract market system and reproduces itself without labour, a world of "now" in which trivial fashion decisions, made in corporate board rooms, reach out to make "a lean winter down on the farm" some long distance away.

It is also a spatial world cut off from historical time, a world spatialized, detemporalized, de-collectivized. It uses a set of calendar markers to link, on a trivial surface level, two isolated, emotionally and spiritually depthless individuals. These are not only the classic representations of commodity consumer society, but they are themselves commodities who consume each other.

Consuming the Code

Sylvie and the speaker as literary characters reveal to us that they have consumed the code of consumerism, been inscribed with the values of consumer society. In their interactions, as these are revealed to us, they constantly reproduce and reinforce the code. To be inscribed by society is to have one's body inhabited by society. The senses may be given by nature, but the form they take, the ways in which the senses mediate between the self and the external world, is culturally structured, just as our language is. Our bodies in this sense are inhabited by society. Arnason has inscribed his characters so fully with the code of consumerism that they are emotionally empty: exteriorities in a society of outsides. We get a sense of all this in the constant use of "in" and "into" and in references to food intake, e.g. sentences (70)-(77).

Elaborated and Restricted Linguistic Codes

The speaker not only echoes literature (see INTERTEXTUALITY, p. 209) but speaks in the measured, precise terms of the elaborated code to reveal that linguistic forms are influenced by print culture (see STEREOTYPE, p. 212). This allows the coolness and distance of an analytical mind to dispense plain prose discourse (undermined by the author through the games with signifiers) in an apparently objective way. The much looser, less precise, more emotional non-standard English Restrictive Code of oral and popular culture appears after the sneering condescension of the speaker when he says "Pappy" in "Sylvie's Pappy phones me up", which introduces Pappy speaking, in sentences (89) to (91), in the restricted code:

> We done run out of moonshine, boy, he tells me. Sure is hot down on them cotton fields without any moonshine. That Remy Martin weren't hardly enough to raise a thirst.

The first sentence is an example of the DIRECT STYLE OF NARRATION in which the speaker relates directly what was said, and indicates through "he tells me" that he is doing so. Arnason presumably leaves the quotation marks off the quoted words to give us a cue that something strange is happening. In the other two sentences the speaker either mockingly mimics, or gets absorbed into Pappy's code, because he speaks half in the written-elaborated, and half in the oral-restricted, code: "Sure is hot down on them cotton fields" is in the restricted code, "without any moonshine", the elaborated. The first is on one register or level of discourse (lower class), the second on another (upper class).

Sylvie has moved (is upwardly mobile) from the restricted code of her rural upbringing into the orbit of the elaborated code. We see this in:

> Tweeds are in, she tells me. There's a fortune to be made in tweeds.

But she also says:

> Cotton's out, she says. Pappy, that slackass old bastard...

Which returns her to her past, to the restricted-oral code of her past and family.

Gemeineschaft and Gesellschaft

Gemeineschaft and Gesellschaft is the title of a book by Ferdinand Tonnies, written in 1887, a date that was the epitome of that period of intense industrialization and political integration of Germany (1870), leading a number of independent states into a politically unified and economically capitalist nation state. In such a rapid process, it was possible for a critical observer to see two different aspects of society existing side by side: the old community-centred, organic community of tradition (GEMEINESCHAFT); and the new urban-inspired society of change and isolated competitive individuals (GESELLSCHAFT). From inside the latter, where we are today, it becomes too easy to idealize the former and look back upon it romantically as a kind of lost golden age. The temptation should be resisted, as Arnason does in "Sylvie". There, the residual elements of the last of the old organic community of the deep South, in the form of Sylvie's father, stand opposite the competitive isolated individualist values of Sylvie and the narrator-speaker, to reveal both as corrupt.

Anomie

Coined by Durkheim to describe the existence of competitive and isolated individuals in modern, mass urban societies, ANOMIE describes the individual in *Gesellschaft* societies. Seen from the point of view of *Gemeineschaft*, or old organic community, more *Gesellschaft* individuals appear to be uncaring, robot-like things. In rural areas today where the *illusion* of community in the old sense persists, anomie, and the anomic, describes what rural folk say when they speak of city folk and their curious ways.

The narrator-speaker lives the anomic existence, and his relationship with Sylvie is a classic example of anomie.

Buber's "I and Thou"

In his book *I and Thou*, German-Jewish neo-Hasidic Martin Buber speaks of two fundamental kinds of human relationships: the I and the Thou, and the I and the It. I-Thou relationships are "authentic" or truly human relationships between caring and equal individuals. I-It relationships are those of power in which the I treats the other as an instrument to be manipulated by the I's instrumental rationality in the interests of domination. Arnason's text pits the I-Thou ideal that is an authentic love relationship against the I-It manipulations of the narrator-speaker, of Sylvie, and of the father (he manipulates to get his "moonshine").

Reification

REIFICATION comes from the Latin (*res*=thing), and means the turning of the biological, the organic and the cultural—humans, nature, books, symphonies—from processes into things. Poetry and prose fiction discourse with an obvious and monological level of meaning leave the reader passive, i.e. do not challenge or change him. The single level reifies both text and reader. In literary criticism, reification means the production of a single unified level of meaning out of classic texts, again to level out (i.e. ignore) the complexities of texts from the past. In music, reification takes the form of the search for a definitive performance, i.e. a single, unified interpretation. This levels the whole of the cultural into a single dimension to produce what Marcuse named, in the title of his book, *One Dimensional Man*. In a world of commodities (polished and sold by advertising) we have the polished and sold definitive musical performance, and so on, to produce a polished and sold consumer. "Sylvie", in a deliberately stylized, repetitive way, not only fights single-levelled realism and the beginning, middle and end approach with its reaffirmation of values, but it deliberately sets out to give us, in the realm of literary discourse, an ironic image of what our world is "really" like, i.e. repeated advertisements, jingles, conversational discourse governed by popular music, so that all become cliché. Arnason does not, of course, sneer at these popular forms from some academic height, but draws out some of their latent implications that allow them to speak in another way. There is, for example, the frequent mention of water and allusions to the Leadbelly song:

> Gimme little water Sylvie
> Gimme little water now
> Gimme little water Sylvie
> Gimme little once in a while.

This obviously speaks of the need for water as the material basis of existence, but it goes on to have very profound symbolic meanings through repetition in "Sylvie" that would take a whole book to explicate: water as source of being (sea), sex, etc.

Eroticism and Phallic Symbolism

The reading of Lewis Carroll's *Bruno and Sylvie* reminded Arnason (he says in conversation), through its images and symbols of eating and penetration, of the highly repressed sexual character of Victorian society, and this is one source of the images of penetration, "in" and "into", and of the food and drink images (on one level) in his "Sylvie".

Subliminal Seduction

Arnason had recently been reading *Subliminal Seduction*, the classic little text on the use of sex in advertising, when he wrote "Sylvie". There the sexual implications of cigarettes and straws in mouths are fully revealed.

Repressive Sublimation and Repressive Desublimation

The text "Sylvie" picks up the Victorian phallicism and eroticism to point to the repressive sublimation of that society. In this view, "undesirable" sexual impulses are repressed and re-channelled to appear in more socially desirable forms, or so the Victorians thought. In fact, these repressed desires and feelings would often invade Victorian prose as a latent and unrecognized level of meaning to produce highly erotic or phallic results just beneath the seriousness of the prose or poetic discourse.

Our society prides itself on having escaped from the repressiveness of the Victorians, but it has, as Marcuse explains in *Eros and Civilization*, only escaped into a world of desublimated repression. Here, sexuality is brought out of the closet and into the open; but only to produce an open, yet concealed, repressiveness where advertisements convert sex into material things in order to profit by selling these "things". The girl is supposed to come with the car. This is precisely the world of "Sylvie".

Non-Specificity of Space and Place

Sylvie goes to Copenhagen, Scotland, and so on, but as her own name signifies an abstract entity without indicating a specific content, so does the naming of the exotic locales to which she travels. This absence of specificity of place and space has its origins in the ideology of advertising and its spatialization of time. As John Berger puts it in his *Ways of Seeing*:

> The entire world becomes a setting for the fulfillment of publicity's promise of the good life. The world smiles at us. It offers itself to us. And because *everywhere* is imagined as offering itself to us, *everywhere* is more or less the same.

Sylvie as Dream

We have no way of knowing whether the speaker in "Sylvie" is awake or asleep; being made by Arnason to consciously muse or have his dream uttered. And in one important way it does not matter, because both worlds are inner worlds which are uttered (which means outered). As dream this could be a full dream or that halfway house between dreaming and waking, a daydream. Daydreams are built into the very structure of the world of advertising with which we are surrounded. Again, as Berger puts it:

> The gap between what publicity actually offers and the future it promises, corresponds with the gap between what the spectator-buyer feels himself to be and what he would like to be. The two gaps become one, and instead of the single gap being bridged by action or lived experience, it is filled with glamorous day-dreams.

This captures with great precision the position of the speaker in "Sylvie", as well as the condition of the world delineated there.

Megavisual and Megaverbal

In his various works (e.g. *Art and Psychoanalysis* and *Aesthetics After Modernism*), Peter Fuller speaks of the megavisual tradition of our time in visual art, and to this we may as well add the megaverbal tradition. In *Aesthetics After Modernism*, he echoes John Berger's classic *Ways of Seeing* when he notes that advertising art is a moribund form of the old Fine Arts tradition which it has largely displaced, for Fine Arts have:

> become only a small strand in what I have treated elsewhere, "the mega-visual tradition" of monopoly capitalism. Here I am referring to such phenomena as photography, mass-printing, billboards, neon signs, television, video, holography, and so on with which we are constantly surrounded. But I believe it is wrong to regard such things as the mode of the aesthetic dimensions in our time...they represent only its occlusion and eclipse.

Arnason's text is a verbal art object which deals with and challenges the megaverbal and megavisual traditions of manipulation by using irony and hyperbole. Through these he creates stereotype characters who are "real" (literary reflections of empirical reality) because we live in an essentially homogenized society where the stereotype has been internalized or inscribed, is "real".

Captains of Consciousness

In his extremely lucid and readable text *Captains of Consciousness*, Stuart Ewen anatomizes the ideology and institutional rise of advertising in twentieth-century Euro-American civilization. The title of the book alludes ironically to the well-known phrase "Captains of Industry", a metaphorical term (captain of the ship) used to designate the new and powerful industrial capitalists of the nineteenth century. Whereas guiding industry was the nineteenth-century aim, guiding the whole of consciousness of all the people became their successors' goal in the twentieth century. The ideological, instrumental means of this enterprise became the new advertising and media networks. By making his characters stereotypes on one level, by having them utter and act out media clichés, Arnason creates a microcosmic textual world which exaggerates only to bring out the essence of our own macrocosm of empirical experience.

The Sane Society

A few lines from *The Sane Society* by Erich Fromm will locate the speaker and Sylvie for us in a larger historical context. Fromm writes:

> Monotheistic religions themselves have, to a great extent, regressed into idolatry. Man projects his power of love and reason unto God; he does not feel them any more as his own powers, and then he prays to God to give him back some of what he, man, has projected unto God. In early Protestantism and Calvinism, the required religious attitude is that man *should* feel himself empty and impoverished, and put his trust in the grace of God, that is, into the hope that God may return to him part of his own qualities, which he has put into God.

> Every act of submissive worship is an act of alienation and idolatry in this sense. What is frequently called "love" is often nothing but the idolatrous phenomenon of alienation; only that not God or an idol, but another person is worshipped in this way. The "loving" person in this type of submissive relationship, projects all his or her love, strength, thought, into the other person, and experiences the loved person as a superior being, finding satisfaction in complete submission and worship.... Just as in the case of religious idolatry, he has projected all his richness into the other person, and experiences this richness not any more as something which is his, but as something alien from himself, deposited in somebody else with which he can get in touch only by submission to, or submergence in the other person.

This world and this "love" is that of "Sylvie".

A Final Note on Closure

Arnason's text "Sylvie" ends (closes) with the word "now". It is simultaneously the "now" of the narrator's textual world; the "now" of the reader at the juncture of finishing the reading of the text and doing something else; and the "now" of the empirical, extra-textual world of reader and writer.

POSTSCRIPT

"Language" is a high level abstraction which finds itself in the world only by means of the development of the mediating discourse forms from which it has been constructed. This language and these discourse forms are never fixed, and thus never final, being subject to the erosions and creations of time. For the present, we seem to be able to distinguish between the two polarities of underdetermined and overdetermined discourse forms, and these, in popular mythology, are supposed to correspond either to fiction (overdetermined) or to non-fiction, the language of Truth (underdetermined). In fact, no discourse form can be truly underdetermined, because semantics or conceptual meaning can never be separated from syntax, and indeed semantics cannot exist at all without syntax. The "facts" associated with the underdetermined discourse of Truth are cultural constructions, created by and bound by the texts which they purport to inform. The boundaries which allegedly separate underdetermined from overdetermined discourse do not therefore exist quite as has been thought, for both forms meet on the common ground of the cultural construction of any text. This means that "facts" and fact-based texts of underdetermined discourse may be fictions in the pejorative sense, while "fictions" may be conveyors of "truth" in the relativist, cultural sense. The lesson to be learned in all this is that which we started with: "The Language of *TIME*". An informed citizenry in the modern age must be able to understand discourse theory and practice as a precondition of their merely being informed. This book has therefore been an attempt at providing the reader with the tools he or she needs so as to be sure, ironically, that he or she is, in fact, informed.

POSTSCRIPT

WORKS CITED

[This list includes only those works cited which the reader may have difficulty locating. Poems and other short works cited in the text and not mentioned specifically here are to be found in the anthologies listed.   K.J.H.]

An Anthology of Canadian Literature in English. 2 vols., ed. Donna Russell and Russell Brown. Toronto: Oxford University Press, 1983.

Aristotle. *Poetics*. Trans. Leon Golden. Englewood Cliffs, N.J.: Prentice-Hall, 1968.

Arnason, David. *The Circus Performers' Bar*. Vancouver: Talon Books Ltd., 1984.

Barthes, Roland. *S/Z*. New York: Hill and Wang, 1974.

Berger, John. *Ways of Seeing*. London: BBC, 1972.

Berger, Peter and Luckmann, Thomas. *The Social Construction of Reality*. New York: Anchor Books, 1967.

Bernstein, Basil. *Class Codes and Control*. London: Routledge and Kegan Paul, 1971.

Brooker, Bertram. *Sounds Assembling*. Winnipeg, Man.: Turnstone Press, 1980.

Buber, Martin. *I and Thou*. Trans. Ronald Gregor Smith. New York: Scribner's, 1958.

Callaghan, Morley. *Such Is My Beloved*. Toronto: McClelland and Stewart, 1957.

Carroll, Lewis. *The Collected Works of Lewis Carroll*. London: Nonsuch, 1939.

Coleridge, Samuel Taylor. *On the Constitution of the Church and State*. London: Hurst, Chance and Co., 1830.

Cooley, Dennis. *Bloody Jack*. Winnipeg, Man.: Turnstone Press, 1985.

de Saussure, Ferdinand. *A Course in General Linguistics*. London: Fontana, 1974.

Dirkheim, Emile. *Suicide*. Translated by J.A. Spaulding and G. Simpson. Glencoe, 1951.

Easthope, Antony. *Poetry as Discourse*. London: Methuen, 1983.

Ewen, Stuart. *Captains of Consciousness*. New York: McGraw Hill, 1976.

Fromm, Erich. *The Sane Society*. New York: Hope, 1955.

Fuller, Peter. *Aesthetics After Modernism*. London: Writers & Readers, 1983.

_____. Art and Psychoanalysis. London: Writers & Readers, 1980.

Georgian Poetry 1911-12. London: Poetry Bookshop, 1912.

Gross, David. "Space, Time and Modern Culture" in *TELOS* 50 (Winter 1981-82).

Haber, Ralph and Hershenson, Maurice. *Psychology of Visual Perception*, 2nd ed. New York: H. Holt & Co., 1980.

Halliday, M.A. and Hasan, R. *Cohesion in English*. White Plains, N.Y.: Longman, 1976.

Harrison, Charles Yale. *Generals Die In Bed* (1930). Hamilton, Ont.: Potlatch Press, 1976.

Hemingway, Ernest. "Hills Like White Elephants" in *The Short Stories of Ernest Hemingway*. New York: Scribner, 1953.

Herrnstein-Smith, Barbara. *Poetic Closure: A Study of How Poems End*. Chicago: University of Chicago Press, 1974.

Hirst, G. "Anaphora in Natural Language Understanding." Thesis, University of British Columbia, 1976.

Thomas Hobbes. *Leviathan*. London: Everyman edition, J.M. Dent & Sons, 1914.

Hobbs, J.R. "Towards an Understanding of Coherence" in *Coherence in Spoken and Written Discourse*, ed. Deborah Tannen. Norwood, N.J.: Ablex Publishing, 1982.

Jackson, Rosemary. *Fantasy*. London: Methuen, 1982.

Jameson, Fredric. *The Political Unconscious*. Ithaca, N.Y.: Cornell University Press, 1981.

Key, Wilson P. *Subliminal Seduction*. New York: New American Library, 1974.

Kroetsch, Robert. *Alibi*. Toronto: Stoddart, 1983.

Kuhn, Thomas. *The Structure of Scientific Revolutions*, 2nd ed. Chicago: University of Chicago Press, 1970.

Lakoff, George and Johnson, Mark. *Metaphors We Live By*. Chicago: University of Chicago Press, 1980.

Lampman, Archibald. *The Poems of Archibald Lampman*, ed. Margaret Coulby Whitridge. Toronto: University of Toronto Press, 1974.

Leacock, Stephen. *Literary Lapses*. Toronto: McClelland and Stewart, 1957.

Leech, Geoffrey. *A Linguistic Guide to English Poetry*. London: Longman, 1969.

Lukacs, Georgi. "The Intellectual Physiognomy of Literary Character" in *Radical Perspectives in the Arts*, ed. Lee Baxandall. New York: Pelican, 1972.

Lyons, John. *Semantics*. 2 vols. Cambridge, Mass.: Cambridge University Press, 1977.

Lyotard, Jean François. *Report on Post-Modern Knowledge*. Minneapolis: University of Minnesota Press, 1984.

Marcuse, Herbert. *Eros and Civilization*. Boston: Beacon Press, 1955.

_____. *One Dimensional Man*. Boston: Beacon Press, 1964.

Marlyn, John. *Putzi I Love You You Little Square*. Toronto: Coach House Press, 1981.

McCullers, Carson. "A Tree, A Rock, A Cloud" in *Story*, ed. Boyd Litzinger and Joyce Carol Oates. Lexington, Mass.: D.C. Heath & Co., 1985.

McLuhan, Herbert Marshall. *Understanding Media*. New York: McGraw, 1964.

Mumford, Lewis. *Technics and Society*. London: Routledge and Kegan Paul, 1932.

Norton Anthology of English Literature. 2 vols. New York: W.W. Norton & Co., 1968.

O'Connor, F. *The Complete Stories*. New York: Farrar, Straus & Giroux, 1971.

Ong, Walter S.J. *Orality and Literacy*. London: Methuen, 1982.

Open Letter. Edited and published by Frank Davey, 104 Lyndhurst Ave., Toronto, Ont. M5R 2Z7

Oxford Dictionary of Quotations. 2nd ed. London: Oxford University Press, 1955.

Parker, Patricia. "The (Self) Identity of the Literary Text" in *Identity of the Literary Text*, ed. Mario J. Valdes and Owen Miller. Toronto: University of Toronto Press, 1985.

Peacham, Henry. *The Garden of Eloquence*. Scholar Press Facsimile (1593), 1977.

Pinter, Harold. *The Birthday Party*. London: Methuen, 1981.

Plato. *Dialogues*. 2 vols., trans. Benjamin Jowett. New York: Random House, 1937.

Poe, Edgar Allan. "The Fall of the House of Usher" in *Story*, ed. Boyd Litzinger and Joyce Carol Oates. Lexington, Mass.: D.C. Heath and Co., 1985.

Pound, Ezra. *Selected Letters 1907-1941*, ed. D.D. Paige. New York: New Directions, 1971.

Rifaterre, Michael. *Semiotics of Poetry*. Bloomington, Ind.: Indiana University Press, 1978.

Ross, Sinclair. *As For Me And My House*. Toronto: McClelland and Stewart, 1957.

————. *The Lamp at Noon and Other Stories*. Toronto: McClelland and Stewart, 1968.

Sinclair, John. "Lines About 'Lines'" in *Language and Literature*, ed. Ronald Carter. London: George Allen and Unwin, 1982.

Sproxton, Birk, ed. *Trace: Prairie Writers on Writing*. Winnipeg, Man.: Turnstone Press, 1986.

Thurber, James. "The Secret Life of Walter Mitty" in *Form and Thought in Prose*, ed. W.H. Stone and Robert Hoopes. New York: Ronald Press Co., 1954.

Tigar, Michael and Levy, Madeline R. *Law and the Rise of Capitalism*. New York: Monthly Review Press, 1977.

Tonnies, Ferdinand. *Community and Society*, trans. C.P. Loomis, New York: Harper, 1963.

Traherne, Thomas. *Centuries, Poems and Thanksgivings*. 2 vols. Oxford at the Clarendon Press, 1958.

Twentieth Century Anthology, ed. W.E. Messenger and W.H. New. Toronto: Prentice-Hall, 1984.

Wilden, Antony. *System and Structure*, 2nd ed. London: Tavistock Publications, 1980.

Williams, Raymond. *Keywords*. London: Flamingo, 1984.

————. *The Long Revolution*. London: Chatto and Windus, 1961.

Wilson, Ethel. *Swamp Angel*. Toronto: McClelland and Stewart, 1962.